They Were Good Germans Once

Also by Evelyn Toynton

Fiction:
Modern Art
The Oriental Wife
Inheritance

Non Fiction:
Jackson Pollock

They Were Good Germans Once:

My Jewish Émigré Family

A Memoir

Evelyn Toynton

Delphinium Books

THEY WERE GOOD GERMANS ONCE

Copyright © 2024 by Evelyn Toynton

Printed in the United States of America

For information, address DELPHINIUM BOOKS, INC.,
1250 4th Street, 5th Floor
Santa Monica, CA 90401
Library of Congress Cataloguing-in-Publication Data is available on request.
ISBN 978-1-953002-38-9
24 25 26 27 28 LBC 5 4 3 2 1

Jacket and interior design by Colin Dockrill

"The duality of German and Jew—two souls within a single body—would preoccupy and torment German Jews throughout the nineteenth century and the first decades of the twentieth."—Amos Elon

"The German-Jewish marriage was a rare event, and rarely has the Jewish partner courted love as in this instance . . . [but] the Jewish-German marriage ended in definitive divorce." —Joseph Taubes

For Joseph Olshan, editor extraordinaire, who talked me
into writing this book and then made it better

PREFACE

When I was a child, I had a sense of my relatives not as foreign *per se* but as having more layers to them than other people. Even their accents—though they all spoke impeccable English, the older ones in particular still had distinct German accents—seemed like a sign of some inner richness; they carried another, mysterious world inside them that marked them out from the Americans around me. Now I can see that they were, in their way, displaced persons, strangers in a strange land, not that they whined or complained about it: they did not bemoan their fate, though when I look back at some of their histories, they would seem to have had sufficient cause. *Trauma* was not a word they would have used, or perhaps even recognized; it did not exist in their vocabulary. Nor did *culture shock*. Maybe they felt they had no right to pity themselves: they were the lucky ones, after all—they had survived, as so many of their friends and relatives had not. Or they may have felt that to give way to grief would be a form of self-indulgence, a lack of that discipline so valued in German culture.

While no one in my grandparents' or parents' generation attempted to pass as Gentiles, it had been many years since they had actively practiced their religion; their whole culture, their entire sense of their identity, was German. And right up until the advent of Hitler, they were patriotic to the core. All the men of the family who were of age to fight in the First World War volunteered for service in the German Army. My two grandfathers, my great-uncle, and several of my second cousins were awarded the Iron Cross and commended for their bravery in battle. One of those cousins died in the fighting in France in 1914, just a few weeks into the war. My father's father suffered a war wound on the Eastern Front that left him with a permanently damaged arm.

Unlike the Eastern European Jews, they had always eaten Apfelstrudel and schnitzel rather than gefilte fish and latkes, and had spoken only German, never Yiddish. I don't remember hearing a single word of Yiddish, except maybe *meshugenneh*, until, when I was nineteen, I became friends with someone who'd been raised in a cramped apartment in Brooklyn with his Yiddish-speaking grandmother, a refugee from the pogroms in her native Russia. Not only was my new friend's speech littered with Yiddish words, but he was deeply suspicious of German Jews—*yekkes*, as Yiddish speakers like his grandmother called them.

Nobody had ever told me before about the class warfare between people like my relatives and his. But *yekkes*, he informed me, considered themselves the aristocracy of Jewry, far more civilized and refined than their co-religionists elsewhere—particularly those "peasants" from the *shtetls* of Eastern Europe, whom they regarded with distaste and distanced themselves from as much as possible. I'd never heard any member of my family express such snobbish views, but as he pointed out, they may have had no occasion to: they probably associated only with other *yekkes*. (Years later, the editor of a distinguished scholarly journal would tell me a riddle about German Jews. Question: "What's the difference between a virgin and a *yekke*?" Answer: "Once a *yekke*, always a *yekke*.")

My friend even darkly suggested that the *yekkes*, along with all their other sins, had been so eager to fend off Bolshevik incursions that they'd supported the Nazis in their early years. No proof of that allegation existed in the history books, so I managed to persuade him that it wasn't true, but in his eyes, even if they'd never colluded with the Nazis, German Jews would always be more German than Jewish. That wasn't something I could argue with, given some of my relations' undeniably German traits: punctuality was a cardinal virtue for them, they placed a very high value on discipline and hard work, their characteristic mode was seriousness. Certainly they weren't given to my friend's exuberant brand of joking and mockery, any more than they went in for immoderate displays of emotion; hugs and extravagant professions of love were not part of their repertoire.

My friend accused me, too, of not being Jewish enough—not only didn't I know any Hebrew, or many Old Testament stories, according to him I didn't look like a Jew, didn't act like one, didn't sound or even laugh like one. Yet he, more than anyone else I'd met, made me feel my Jewishness as intrinsic to who I was, as though some buried part of me were coming to the surface. Once, after spending an afternoon listening to an acquaintance from Tennessee describe her frontier ancestors and the quilts her family had handed down from generation to generation, I phoned him and said, "I just realized something: I'm a Yid." And he said, "I know that, but if you never say it loudly enough, no one else will ever figure it out."

While his grandmother had told him in harrowing detail about the Cossacks rampaging through the *shtetl*, no member of my family ever talked to me about what the Nazis had done. I wonder how much, in my early childhood, right after the war, they thought of those other Jews, the ones who'd perished in the camps, or in mobile gas vans, or at the trenches the *Einsatzgruppen* made them dig before shooting them en masse—both the ones they had known and all those millions they hadn't. Even later, when books on the Holocaust began appearing in great numbers in America, I don't remember seeing a single one on their bookshelves. At the age of ten, I read *The Diary of Anne Frank*, but not because any member of the older generation had mentioned it; my sister heard about it from a friend and, after reading it herself, passed it on to me. Though we talked about it endlessly between ourselves, and I had nightmares for months afterward about the Nazis coming for us, we never mentioned the subject to our parents. It would have felt cosmically tactless to remind people who had lived through that time of what the Germans had done. It was not a subject to be discussed outside our bedroom—it was too scary, too dangerous.

So many of the Nazi-era stories I tell in this book, the back stories of my relations who came of age in Germany, I learned long after their deaths. Most of the real horrors happened to people I never knew well, or people who died before I was born or when I was very young. In those cases, it is their widows, some of whom I did know well, who form the subject of the memoirs collected here. But what happened to their husbands was so much a part of their story that to describe them without relating what they had gone through before I knew them would be to strip away much of what made them who they were.

CHAPTER ONE: *Mothers and Daughters*

My grandmother may be as responsible as the Nazis for my mother's inability to stand up for herself when her fate depended on it. My mother learned the habit of submission at such an early age that when it came time for her to fight for her rights, she meekly accepted the judgment of others on what she was entitled to, with disastrous consequences.

I cannot remember my grandmother as anything but an old lady, with witchy white hair sprouting from her chin and above her lip in a way that fascinated me as a child, and that now makes me check my own face regularly for such growths. Nor can I remember her smiling, except very rarely, such as when she beat me at Chinese checkers, our main pastime together. These games took place at the small round table in the foyer of her shabby apartment in Inwood, a largely German Jewish neighborhood in upper Manhattan, where I, too, lived for my first nine years. We talked very little at those times, concentrating hard on the worn board between us. My grandmother was not given to telling me stories about her life before she arrived in America, though there would have been many stories to tell.

She had begun life as the daughter of a rich industrialist, a stern paterfamilias who had rigid ideas about the role of women. And so, although women were already being accepted, in however small numbers, at German universities, he refused to allow my grandmother to attend, though she had been the star pupil at her school. Her brother, her one sibling, was a different matter: he was not only allowed to get a university education, it was impressed on him that his father expected and demanded that he excel at his studies. When he failed an examination—he may have been less intellectually gifted than my grandmother—he killed himself rather than face his father's wrath. In the living room of the apartment where those games of Chinese checkers took place was a large, handsomely framed portrait of this brother. But only from my mother did I learn what had become of him.

How my grandmother had managed to get that painting out of Germany in 1939 is a mystery, though she had also brought with her a number of tablecloths richly embroidered with peacocks and dragons and swans, and stacks of linen kitchen towels, each still neatly held together with lavender ribbon, each with her married initials on them and marked for a distinct purpose: some were for plates, others for glasses; there were even separate ones for forks as opposed to spoons. There were also evening bags, elaborately beaded and encrusted, swaddled in ancient tissue paper. None of these relics of a once affluent existence was ever used in America; when

she died, we discovered them, in tidy piles, in the wardrobe in her bedroom, along with several Galle vases and
wooden packing boxes containing a complete set of
Limoges china, edged in gold; my older sister and I divid-
ed all these expensive things between us. My grandmother
must have had to forfeit any number of even more valuable
things when she left Germany, to be allowed to take those
remnants of her former life with her.

If she never told us about her brother, she also never
mentioned her husband, who had emigrated with her but
died when I was just two years old. Theirs had not been a
love match. My grandfather's beloved younger sister was
engaged to be married, but could not afford a dowry, and
so my grandfather married my rich grandmother in order
to provide her with one. It doesn't speak very well for his
character, yet my mother adored him, just as he adored
her, which was the root of the problem in that household.
My grandmother must have realized that her witty and
charming husband had not married her for love, that he
much preferred their daughter to her; she was ferociously
jealous of my mother, though my mother was vague about
the details of the form that jealousy took. The full story
was only told to me after my mother's death, by her cousin, the son of my grandfather's brother: they had lived
next door to each other in Fuerth, an industrial city not
far from Nuremberg, and both being only children, had
been more like brother and sister than cousins, seeing
each other every day.

It seems that my grandmother's dislike of my mother did not stop at coldness or other forms of emotional punishment. She was furious that my mother was left-handed, and tried to force her to use her right hand instead, though she never entirely succeeded; when she caught her writing with the wrong hand during her school years, she would hit her repeatedly with a belt. Nor were those the only times when she resorted to physical force. "She beat her terribly when she was in a rage," her cousin told me. "We all knew about it, but what could we do back then? Nowadays, she would have been reported for child abuse."

My mother escaped as often as possible to her cousin's house, where his parents made much of her; it was generally agreed that she had inherited her father's charm and humor, the two things my grandmother signally lacked. (During the famine that followed the First World War in Germany, my mother told me how she and her father would go out into the countryside together, to try to barter with farmers for food; they never took her mother along, she told us, because part of their success was due not just to the valuable objects they had to offer but to their ability to win the farmers over, and her mother would have been hopeless at that.)

By the time my mother was sixteen, her father was so alarmed by the situation at home that he sent her to a finishing school in Switzerland, ostensibly so that she could perfect her French, but really to get her away from my grandmother. Afterward, in order to perfect her English as well, she took a three-month job as an *au pair* in London; the idea was that at the end of that period, she would return to Germany. But the year was 1933; her father wrote to her in February and told her not to come back. She never set foot in Germany again.

My grandfather had fought in the German Army during World War I, as had his brother, and both had been awarded the Iron Cross, but that didn't protect them from the rising anti-Semitism of the Nazi years. They were in business together; they had a mill that produced woolen cloth, which had provided them with a modest but adequate income until the rampant inflation of the '20s and later the Depression that began in 1929. In the mid-'30s, they decided to move to Munich, which, although it was Hitler's base at the time, they felt was less completely Nazified than Fuerth. In 1935, like all the other Jews in Germany, they had been deprived of their German citizenship by the Nuremberg Laws, and their business had been "Aryanized" —sold for a very low price to a German Gentile—but presumably whatever was left of my grandmother's fortune was enough to enable them to scrape by.

Then, in November 1938, came Kristallnacht. My grandparents' furniture was smashed up, as was that of almost every Jewish household that night: the old-fashioned German clock—known, ironically, as a grandmother clock, being half the size of a grandfather one—that had also hung in my grandmother's apartment, and now hangs

11

in my house in England, has a deep indentation in the wood; the man who cleaned and serviced the clock for me a few years ago told me it had been made by an axe.

The furniture was not the only victim of the damage that night. My grandfather and great-uncle were arrested, along with nearly thirty thousand other Jewish men, and taken to Dachau, where they remained for almost two months. Despite their having been "front fighters" in the war, which supposedly entitled them to be released early, they were sent home only when they both got typhoid, and the guards were afraid of catching it themselves. My great-uncle was in such bad shape that my grandfather, weak as he was, had to carry him home to Munich, where he was put to bed by his wife and died a few days later. Somehow my grandfather survived, and in 1939 my father, already married to my mother, managed to find a sponsor for them, which entitled them to emigrate to America.

On arrival in New York, they moved to Inwood, into the apartment where I would visit my grandmother for the first twenty-five years of my life, and opened a dry cleaning establishment with what little money they had managed to take out of Germany. Although my grandfather's health had never been good since his time in Dachau, he worked there until his death in 1950, after which my grandmother sold it. (No doubt what happened to his daughter in America two years before his death also contributed to the heart attack that killed him.) The great irony is that for over twenty years, my mother and grand-mother were each other's most frequent companions; having nobody else to spend their birthdays and Christmas with, they always spent them together. They were locked in a communion that my mother suffered rather than en-joyed.

But if not exactly a doting granny—it was not in her nature—my grandmother was never unkind to me and my sister the way she had been to my mother. She used to buy little cakes from the bakery for our visits, and turn on the electric heater when I came in winter, because as she helped me off with my coat, she always remarked on how cold my hands were. I remember her as constantly sniff-ing, constantly twisting her own hands fretfully in her lap, but as a child, I never thought to interpret these behaviors as a sign of discontent; they were simply part of who she was. And sometimes, *a propos* of nothing in particular, she would suddenly brighten, she'd grow animated, and ask me if I'd like to hear a comic song in Bavarian dialect, one she'd learned from a servant who had come from the countryside to work in her father's household. "*Meine madel ist eine Milliladel*," it began, or at least that's how I remember it. Each time she asked me if I wanted to hear it, I'd act as though she'd never sung it for me before.

She had one friend in New York, a fellow refugee named Emmy, whom she'd known since her school days, and every time she mentioned her to me, she would tell me how it was Emmy's fault that she had never really

13

learned to speak French properly. Emmy, she told me, had lured her out to play tennis when she should have been studying her French. I am not sure how many times this happened, but she held a grudge against Emmy well into her eighties.

Not only had Emmy's husband being taken to Dachau on Kristallnacht, and beaten to death there, but she herself had been knocked down the stairs by an SA man that night, and broken both her hip and her leg, so that she never walked without limping, or without pain, again. And her two sons, who had been sent away to Paris in the late '30s, and gone into hiding when the Germans occupied France, were betrayed by an informer and sent to their death in Auschwitz. Yet all my grandmother ever said about Emmy was that she had prevented her from perfecting her French.

Like certain of my other relatives, my grandmother's persecution at the hands of the Nazis had not expunged her conviction that Germany was a superior country to every other, perhaps to America most of all. The very fact that it snowed in the spring in America, she said, was because the mountains were facing in the wrong direction, though I'm not sure what she meant by that—that in Germany the mountains were correctly positioned, and so it never snowed in spring? She also objected to the fact that Israel, in which she otherwise took little interest, had adopted Hebrew as its national language: "It would be so much more civilized if they all spoke German."

At the age of eighty-eight, she was mugged just outside her apartment building; rather than giving up her handbag, she struggled with her attacker, who knocked her to the ground, breaking both her hips. She never recovered. When I went to see her in the hospital, she took my hand and murmured, "Such cold hands—always such cold hands," her usual complaint. But as she was dying, she said it with real fondness; there was more love in her voice than I had ever heard there before. She even tried to rub warmth into my hands with her own two, though they were almost as cold.

Only after she died did we discover not just the treasure trove in the bedroom wardrobe but also the fact that she had been quietly investing in the stock market for years, and left my mother, her only heir, something in the region of $300,000—a tidy sum for 1974. My mother had had no more idea that this money existed than had anyone else; none of us had ever seen a copy of *Barron's* or the *Wall Street Journal* in my grandmother's apartment; we had never heard her mention the stock market. We had always imagined that she was barely scraping by, as had her neighbors: after her death, the woman who lived across the hall told my mother, sighing, "I always felt sorry for that poor woman, she was so shabby, and she didn't even have a proper winter coat." It was a modest version of the story of Hetty Green and her hidden millions.

In her haste to clear out the apartment, my mother allowed anybody who strayed in to take whatever they wanted (apart from the riches in the wardrobe); one woman, whose name my mother didn't even know, took a fancy to the painting of my grandmother's brother and carried it off. It was one of the few times in my adult life that I was truly cross with my mother: knowing what the portrait must have meant to my grandmother—it was the one painting she had brought with her from Germany, the only one hanging on her walls—it seemed callous to have let it go to someone who had no idea of its history. "Did you even tell her who it was?" I asked accusingly, and my mother shook her head, No. "I wish you'd saved it for me," I said: now that it was gone, I felt protective of it, full of an almost yearning tenderness for the young man who had died seventy years before. I suspected that the woman who'd taken it had really only wanted the old-fashioned gilt frame, or just liked the idea of hanging the portrait of a well-dressed young man in her apartment, which was no doubt as shabby as my grandmother's.

But my mother, who had lived with that painting throughout her childhood, who perhaps had been told that she could never compensate for the loss of that much-loved brother (my grandmother must have hoped for a son she could name after him), had apparently felt no sentiment about it, just as she never reminisced sentimentally about my grandmother after her death. Probably her main emotion was relief. She had intended, when she left for England, to escape from her mother for good once she returned; her plan was to get an apartment in Munich, get a job teaching French or English, so that her real life could begin.

But then Hitler became chancellor, and she got that letter from her father, telling her not to return. He could not send her money, the German government having imposed harsh currency restrictions; he could only smuggle a few Deutschmarks hidden between the sheets of his letters. The Depression was worldwide; unemployment was rampant in England; she could not get a permit to work as anything except a "domestic"—a servant. She managed to find a job as a maid in a household in Kensington, but physically weak as she was, from growing up in the post-war famine in Germany, she proved incapable of carrying out the tasks expected of her. She had to beg one of the other maids to help her when it was her turn to flip the mattresses, she could not shove the furniture around to sweep behind it. One morning she fainted as she was trying to carry a heavy coal scuttle up a flight of stairs; the coal went tumbling down to the floor below, and she was fired. It was then that a kindly man at the resident aliens' office told her that the category of domestics included governesses. By lying about certain of her credentials—she did not tell the agency where she applied for a post that she had failed math at her school in Fuerth, where she'd been taught by Henry Kissinger's father—she landed a job as governess to a sickly young boy on an estate in Kent, where she stayed for five whole years and fell in love with the English countryside and English history.

Every night, she told me, she had to study up on the math she would be doing with her charge the following day, but at least she was able to teach him French as well as German, and his kindly parents were very pleased with her. The father worked in the Foreign Office, and in his letters her own father would urge her to tell her employer that Germany was rearming, which she did, but she was never sure how seriously the man took these warnings from his son's young governess.

Somehow she must have managed to get to London quite a lot, maybe when her charge went with his family to their summer home in Scotland, because during the period she was working in Kent, she met enough young men to get "engaged" six times. (I can only think that when people wanted to sleep together in those days, they got engaged, or thought of themselves as engaged.) Once, she told me, she had to jump off a ship in the Mediterranean to avoid a young man who was pursuing her. Another time, she and her cousin Lottie, the daughter of the aunt whose dowry had been purchased with her mother's money, went to Paris together and discovered when their long weekend was up that they had just enough money left either to eat a meal or to buy return tickets. They opted for the tickets.

All these stories, which she recounted with wry amusement, made her sound like a total flibbertigibbet, which I believe she was back then, governess or no. When my father's elder brother told my sister and me as teenagers that we would never be as charming and beautiful as our mother, I wasn't insulted or hurt; I was thrilled, just as I was thrilled by the story of her jumping off the ship. I loved imagining her as high-spirited and flirtatious, not the timid woman sitting alone day after day in her dark apartment, with her crippled arm permanently folded across her chest, her shambling walk, her slurred speech, the only way I had ever known her.

Her last engagement during her years in England was to a journalist who landed an assignment to report on the aftermath of a devasting flood in California and persuaded his paper to let her accompany him as his "secretary." In March 1938, they set off for America together, having conceived of a romantic plan to get married when they reached the West Coast. But as they traveled across the country, my mother realized, somewhere in the Rockies, that her intended was a drunk, she'd made a terrible mistake, she couldn't possibly marry him. In Colorado, while he was sleeping off a hangover, she got off the train, leaving a note for him, and wired her cousin from Fuerth, who'd emigrated to the United States the year before: Could he please find some way to get her to New York, where he was living? He borrowed the money for the ticket from his apartment mate and she moved in with the two of them, sleeping on their living room couch, her plan being to earn enough money to return to her beloved England. Somehow—it must have been her charm that did it—she got a job selling gloves at Lord & Taylor and started putting away part of her salary every week.

But she never did get back to England. Her cousin's roommate was my father, seemingly an unlikely mate for her, since he was the most serious of men, and she the most frivolous of women; it must have been the old story of opposites attracting.

He was already working for the company he would remain with, and later serve as head of, all his life, and by the end of that year, when they got married, he had attained enough responsibility to be sent to Cuba on a business trip, so they had their honeymoon there. I have a photograph of them, both beaming, she in a fashionable hat, holding a bunch of flowers, he smiling in a way I would almost never see him smile in the years I knew him.

They, too, lived in Inwood, in an apartment not far from the one my grandparents moved to when they arrived, but at that time my grandfather was still alive, so that, for my mother, it was not such a hardship to be in contact with her parents. (My older sister remembers our grandfather taking her to the local park and plucking bananas for her that he had hidden in the trees, telling her they were banana trees.)

And I believe the newlyweds were genuinely happy. My mother once said, "One of your father's friends said to me after we married that, before, your father had seemed like everyone's grandfather; now he only seemed like everyone's father." When she was still working at Lord & Taylor, she told him she was going to treat him to dinner at a fancy restaurant downtown for his birthday, but when the check came, she realized she didn't have nearly enough money to pay it. So he had to pay for his own birthday dinner. And later, she got into such debt, buying hats and shoes and embossed stationery and French pastries to serve to their guests, that my father had to take a second job for a while, working at night in order to pay off her bills. "I would have been very angry," my uncle said, "but your father thought it was funny; he spoiled her terribly, he never got annoyed with her, or even tried to put her on a budget."

They knew, of course, what was going on back in Germany, as much as anybody could know, but at least most of their close relatives had gotten out—some to America, others to England or Palestine. Then the war broke out, and there was no more news. Only much later did my father find out that his uncle, his mother's brother, had shot himself on the Swiss border, having been refused entry because of the "J" stamped in his passport. Later still, my mother learned that her beloved aunt, the mother of her companion on that trip to Paris, had died in the back of a mobile gas van. I must have been all of thirty when she told me that, or of her father's experiences in Dachau, and his brother's death; up until then, all of the stories she chose to tell me were comic ones.

Owing to his flat feet and extremely poor eyesight, my father was rejected for military service once America entered the war, so they went on living in the apartment in Inwood. The fact that they did not have their first child, my sister, until 1945 may or may not have had something to do with uncertainty about how the war would end, some fear that the Axis might win. But whatever the reason, my mother quit work and spent her days looking after her daughter, who was such an easy child, always gurgling happily, always sleeping through the night after the first month she was home, that she told me the other mothers in their building used to say to her, "She's not a baby, she's an angel. I hope you get a real devil next time."

In 1948, when she was pregnant with me, she started having painful headaches, so fierce that at times she thought her head was about to explode. A series of doctor's appointments followed, at the last of which she was told that she had a tumor pressing on her brain. It was benign, they said, it wouldn't kill her directly, but if it started encroaching on other parts of her brain, not only would the headaches get much worse, it would also affect her eyesight; it could even interfere with her ability to speak, or to recognize words when she heard them. No one could predict with any certainty how fast it would grow, or how much it would affect her functioning, but the doctor told her that if they'd discovered it earlier—she was six months pregnant by the time it was diagnosed—he would have advised a medical abortion: there was no saying how the growth in her brain might affect her baby.

The doctors left it to my father—the man of the house, the one assumed to be equipped to make such decisions—to say whether they should operate or not; even now brain surgery is a risky affair, and in 1948 it was infinitely more dangerous. But he went and spoke to a Dr. Leo Davidoff, a man regarded as the most brilliant neurosurgeon in New York City, maybe in the whole country—a man whose honors, "most of major importance, were so numerous and of such prodigious scope that to cite all of them would constitute too formidable a task," according to one of his obituarists. He was even elected "an honorary member of the American Society of Neuroradiology—an unprecedented manifestation of his recognition as the 'doyen' in this field, a signal honor never before bestowed on a nonradiologist."

Having looked at the X-rays of my mother's brain, Dr. Davidoff told my father it should be possible to remove the tumor without damaging the brain itself. His fees were very steep, however, befitting his stature in the medical community, so my father, whose only debts up to then had been those incurred by my mother, borrowed thousands of dollars from his employer and his elder brother, whom he'd also gotten out of Europe in 1939.

And then I was born, a very long and messy business, with much loss of blood. Several weeks later, the brilliant surgeon operated on my mother. Another obituarist wrote of him that "he was blessed with a manual dexterity in his neurosurgical endeavors that had to be observed to be believed. The house staff members in the hospital (even other than the neurosurgical residents) made it a point to observe Dr. Davidoff operate on at least one occasion, and the awe that they displayed was of poignant interest. He never hurried, but he wasted no time. As a result, he would require two to three hours for a complicated neurosurgical procedure that at the very least would occupy another man on his faculty a minimum of eight hours. This was surgical legerdemain accomplished with what appeared to be a minimum of effort—a reflection of his extraordinary surgical skill." But his manual dexterity, his surgical legerdemain, his extraordinary surgical skill failed him on this occasion. After he'd finished operating on my mother, he came into the waiting room, still in his scrubs, to report to my father that the surgery had not gone as well as he'd hoped; in removing the tumor, which perhaps had been attached to the brain tissues more "stickily" than he'd thought, he had damaged some of the minor arteries, and a hemorrhage had occurred. He could not say yet exactly what effect that would have on my mother's functioning, but he knew that she would be impaired in some way.

"You don't have to pay me," he told my father, who said, "I sent you the check this morning." This was a story my mother told me more than once, with great pride, full of admiration for my father's integrity, his extraordinarily principled conduct. Even the first time she told me, it made me uneasy, though only later could I parse the reasons for my reaction. If he had said, "All right," if he had said, "Don't cash the check," he would have had the means to get expert help for my mother—physiotherapy, speech therapy: all of those things already existed then, but they were never provided for her. The small fortune my father had borrowed went to the surgeon instead. And Dr.

Davidoff, as my mother once told me with a rare show of bitterness, had never shown up at her bedside after the operation: it was only to my father he apologized, not to the woman whose life he had destroyed.

More money had to be borrowed to hire a nanny, a housekeeper, someone who could serve in both roles, since there was no room, in the small apartment where they were living, for more than one person to move in. Before my mother's operation, my father had already gone to an agency and hired a widow from Maine, whose lobsterman husband had died in a boating accident. This woman was to become my surrogate mother for the first five years of my life, and I adored her, just as she adored me—despite the fact that I was a fussy, colicky baby, a bad sleeper from the time I was born, exactly the devil my mother's neighbors had wished for her.

For nine months after my mother's operation, she returned to the apartment, where Aunt Ray, as I called her from the time I could speak, was running things. My mother's left arm—despite my grandmother's best efforts, she had remained left-handed all her life till then—was crippled; her speech was slow and slurred; she had no sight in one eye; her balance was poor. There were veins bulging visibly in her forehead. Though her capacity to think and read was intact, and her speech improved over time, none of the physical damage caused by the surgery would ever be wholly erased. She could not hold me unless someone placed me in the crook of her right arm, and as she told me many years later, Aunt Ray was rarely willing to go to that trouble. The woman I loved like no other when I was a child was not, it seemed, the soul of kindness to everyone that she was to me. "She wanted to get rid of me," my mother said sadly. "She didn't want me there all the time, watching her. So she started telling your father lies about me; she said I shouted at your sister, she said I had threatened to throw you down the incinerator. And he believed her; she was all sweetness and light with him, so respectful, so accommodating, she knew how to turn him against me."

It was this threat to throw me down the incinerator, which my mother swore she never made—and I believe her—that convinced my father she had to be sent away lest she harm me or my sister. And so, once again without consulting her, he found a place on Long Island, essentially just a boarding house where a woman took in relatives people wanted out of the way. Most of them were drying-out drunks. And for over three years my mother was left to her own devices there; my father went to visit her once a month; in the beginning he took my three-year-old sister with him, but that stopped after my sister said, "I don't like this new mommy, I want my old mommy back." She was frightened, too, by the weird men talking to themselves in the parlor where the residents received their visitors.

In the photographs of my sister from those years, she has a lost, bewildered look; until she was three years old she had spent every day with my mother; photographs of them together from that time always show them smiling, laughing, sometimes at the camera and sometimes at each other. Weather permitting, they would go to the park, and to the playground, where my mother pushed her on the swings; my mother brought cookies for her, wrapped in wax paper, in case she got hungry; they went shopping for groceries together, my sister pushing the shopping trolley when it was empty and holding my mother's hand when it was full and she could no longer steer it. At night my mother read her a story and tucked her into bed and kissed her good night. It had been a time in which my sister felt perfectly secure.

Now the mother who'd been the center of that life was gone, and even when she was there, she was not the same woman. And, for whatever reason, Aunt Ray did not adore my sister the way she did me; apparently whenever the two of us got in any sort of trouble, or even if I fell and hurt myself on the playground when we were together, Aunt Ray blamed her; she would scold her and smack her. All her love was lavished on me.

The pain it gave to my mother to be separated from this daughter of hers, with whom she used to spend every day, and from her new baby, whom she had also loved from the start, I cannot begin to imagine.

When my mother had been at the house on Long Island for two and a half years, my father, on one of his visits, told her he wanted a divorce. And because, he said, he didn't want his daughters to hear some sordid story one day about

27

his being caught in a hotel room with a prostitute—adultery being the only grounds for divorce in New York State at the time—he asked her to go to Reno, the divorce capital of America, for six weeks, in order to establish residency and file for divorce there.

I can only assume that whatever frail self-confidence my mother had ever had had been predicated on her charm and beauty; once those were gone, she must have had very little sense of her own worth, or surely she would have protested at some of my father's demands; surely she would have refused to spend six miserable, lonely weeks in a boarding house in Reno to preserve his spotless reputation. But instead of telling him how cruel it was to ask such a thing, she did as he'd requested. Nor, when she had to get a lawyer to process the papers for her, did she argue with the amount of the settlement my father had proposed through his own lawyer: she knew, she said, that he was still paying back the money he'd borrowed to pay the surgeon, and anyway she was sure that the amount he was offering was fair, he being such a fair person. When she told this story, she sounded sorrier for him than she did for herself.

It seems there was no thought on anybody's part of her getting custody of her children; maybe, in those days, no judge would have granted custody to a brain-damaged, physically incapacitated mother. Whatever the truth of the matter, she did not even raise the issue with the court; my father was appointed our sole guardian. On her return from Nevada, he told her, he would find an apartment for her in the city; on the monthly allowance he'd give her, she could pay her rent and cover her daily living expenses. Once she was settled, she would also get some visitation rights. I am not sure what provisions were made in their discussions then, but perhaps the prospect of being able to see her children again made her more amenable to his requests of her.

My father had made no mention of getting remarried, and the idea had not occurred to my mother, but the proprietor of the boarding house on Long Island told her that she shouldn't be so naïve: of course he wanted to get married again; why else would he need a divorce? And that woman was right: my father was planning to marry a secretary from his office, an Italian American Catholic just a few years younger than my mother. In fact, the wedding took place that summer, while my sister and I were in Maine with Aunt Ray, who had been taking us to her run-down house at the easternmost tip of the state every summer for the past four years, my father being concerned to spare us the fierce heat of the city in July and August.

There was no electricity or running water in the house in Bucks Harbor, no plumbing—only an outhouse with three holes of different sizes—but to us it was Paradise. Behind the house was an overgrown apple orchard of splayed, hollowed-out trees, the tall grass between them filled with tangled wildflowers in purple and red and yellow, out of which we made endless bouquets to present to Aunt Ray, and every night we sat on the crumbling wall behind it and watched the sun set. Even now I cannot step into an orchard without feeling a surge of joy, partly mixed with pain; of all the places I have ever known, it's the one most deeply imprinted on what I can only call my soul.

It was my last summer of pure innocence, my Fern Hill. When we returned just before Labor Day, as usual, we found we had a new stepmother, and Aunt Ray wouldn't be living with us any longer. She cried as she said good-bye to me, and I clung to her skirts, begging her not to leave, but it was no use. Our new life had begun.

But that new life also included visits to my mother, in her small apartment six blocks away, and thus began my relationship with her. I turned five that fall, and started in the kindergarten of the local public school, but I have no memory of what I learned there. What I do remember are the stories my mother told us on our visits to her dark little apartment—all of them stories of English kings and queens. By the time I was six, I could name all the wives of Henry VIII, and even knew, for example, that after their divorce, Anna of Cleves used to have eel pies prepared for him when he visited her in her house on the Thames, because he was especially fond of them. By the time I was seven, I knew that Shakespeare, whom I had never read, had been terribly unfair to Richard III, who had actually been a good, kind king, and had nothing to do with the murder of the little princes (it was the Tudor usurper Henry VII who had done it; Horace Walpole had proved that back in the eighteenth century. Shakespeare was forced to create the libel of the evil hunchback because he was writing the play when a Tudor queen sat on the throne). I knew about Lady Jane Grey's sad fate, to which she had been led by scheming courtiers who wanted to pronounce her queen so they could rule in her stead. All those stories, told by my mother in a way that made each royal personage seem realer than real, became a part of my imaginative universe in a way no others did, not even *Anne of Green Gables*.

I learned, too, how to make cups of tea; although my mother could perform such simple tasks herself, having taught herself to use her right hand, she was slower and clumsier at getting things done than I was. It was easier for me to do it, and to bring the tea to her in the living room, where she sat in the green armchair in the corner, with a little rickety table beside her. And I knew that if the tea was made quickly, in the cheap pink plastic cups that were her only china, the next story would come sooner. My sister, being eight by then, was more inclined to go find friends to play with, but I was perfectly happy to sit in the pink chair opposite my mother and go on listening. Or we would play word games together, like Hangman, or do crossword puzzles, at which my mother excelled.

My stepmother never told stories or played games—she made rules instead, and enforced them with threats of punishment—whereas at my mother's there was only one rule I can remember: if I wanted to eat the cookies bought that week by the woman who came to clean and shop for her, I had to eat a "proper" meal first (generally some form of TV dinner, which my mother warmed up in the oven; since she had only one functioning arm, any more complicated cooking was beyond her).

Looking back, I can see that by the time I was six, I had come to associate England with love so completely that I could never disconnect the two in my mind. As I grew older, my Anglophilia migrated more and more from English history to English literature, but my romantic feelings for England had been planted in me at such a young age that even the sometimes disillusioning reality of living here, as I have now done for over twenty years, hasn't rid me of them entirely.

My mother only occasionally read more serious works of history; much of her knowledge of kings and queens was gained from novels that turned them into gorgeous romantic characters, full of dialogue that couldn't possibly have come from the historical record. There was one writer in particular—the sort George Eliot would undoubtedly have included in her scornful condemnation of silly lady novelists—called Margaret Campbell Barnes, who was my mother's particular favorite; by the time I was eight, she was mine, too. Though her books might have been considered inappropriate for children at the time, their allusions to sex were so discreet and vague that nobody could possibly have learned the facts of life from them. After my mother's death I saved the one we both loved best from her bookshelf in the nursing home. Called *Brief Gaudy Hour*, it's about Anne Boleyn, and begins, "Nan! Nan! Come in and be fitted for your new dresses to go to court!" . . . "Yet the girl to whom she called still lingered on the terrace watching the giddy flight of butterflies above the drowsing knott garden. For her, as for them, the gaudy hour of life was being born. Bright as their painted wings, heady as the hot perfume of the flowers."

So: not exactly an example of high art. I couldn't read it now, not even for love of my mother, but at the time it seemed a thrilling revelation of all the richness and tragedy of life. Nor did it occur to me, until many years later, that those long-dead kings and queens, with their stormy passions and stormy tempers and wicked intrigues—"English history is one long string of outrages," my mother said delightedly—were my mother's chief companions, her only escape from the bleakness of her life. If it weren't for them, what would she have had to think about in the silence of her apartment, except the misery of the past few years? My grandfather was dead by then; she saw her mother, dutifully, once a week; she sometimes saw my sister and me twice a week, but not always; the rest of the time, she was sitting in her green armchair by herself, next to a window that looked out at a brick wall.

As we grew older, she started telling us other stories, not from books but from her own happier past, the stories of those adventures in England, and then some from her marriage, always speaking of my father with shy fondness, as though uncertain that she had any right to talk about him at all. Certainly, she never expressed any bitterness toward him, or mentioned my stepmother except in praise of her competence. She was proud of my father's success in business—the promotions kept coming—and told the story of his paying the surgeon with a kind of wonder in her voice. Until we were adults, she never made any reference at all to that house full of drying-out drunks on Long Island, or the trip to Reno, and when she did, it was only very briefly, in passing.

Then we moved to Connecticut with our father and stepmother and my younger brother, their son, and began coming to New York every other weekend to visit my mother. Her single bed, covered with a pink chenille spread, was in the little alcove in the apartment; in the living room was a green couch that opened out into a double bed, and that was where we slept. My sister being a sound sleeper, and I a bad one, like my mother, I sometimes went and sat on her bed in the middle of the night, and we had whispered conversations, or I recited the poems I was learning in school, or ones I had written myself, which she exclaimed over and asked me to write out for her. When she died, I found copies of them still preserved in her battered desk, along with pictures of her I had never seen before: they had been taken for a modeling agency when she first came to New York. I don't believe she ever got a modeling job, but she certainly looked the part, especially in the elegant profile shots, where she was glancing over her shoulder with a teasingly flirtatious look.

34

After years of adoring her, my attitude changed abruptly when I hit adolescence: with her shambling walk, her clothes that never seemed to fit right, the veins bulging in her forehead, she became a source of embarrassment. Whereas once we had gone to the movies together on Saturday afternoons, at the local Loew's theater on Dyckman Street—films like *An Affair to Remember*, *Three Coins in the Fountain*, *Les Girls*, the sort of romances that were to both our tastes—I no longer wished to be seen in public with her. I was afraid of my stepmother, afraid in a different way of my father; the only person I wasn't afraid of was my mother, who was even more powerless than I was. And so she got the full brunt of my teenage surliness, heightened by the rage I carried about my life in the house in Connecticut, though I never told her what was going on there: there was nothing she could have done about it if I had.

No longer content to talk about Richard III or Anna of Cleves's eel pies, or to do crossword puzzles, I spent hours shut in the little dressing room next to the bathroom, where the phone was, talking to the friend I had made at an artsy summer camp the previous summer. If my mother called through the door that she had to use the bathroom, I would shout at her to wait a minute. Sometimes, after my sister left for college, and I was visiting my mother on my own for the weekend, I went to my friend's house in Long Island on Saturday morning, and hardly came back until it was time to catch the train to Connecticut. When I wasn't on the phone, or in Hempstead, I would lock myself in the dressing room and rummage through the closet there for the few relics I could find from my mother's former life. I'd adorn myself in a green silk blouse, a pair of black satin sandals, a square jade ring, and parade around the tiny space, admiring myself in the mirror, but I never had the kindness to go into the living room and strut around in my borrowed finery for my mother's amusement.

If my mother knocked on the door and told me supper was ready—another TV dinner she had warmed up—I'd tell her I wasn't hungry, and anyway I didn't feel like eating that stuff. I'd go out, slamming the door behind me, and return with potato chips and pretzels I'd bought at the local store, which I'd eat in front of her without offering her any. I was such a little bitch that at one point she timidly suggested that perhaps I should visit every third weekend instead of every second one. I can't remember now when I began to feel ashamed of my cruelty, but I suspect that it took more years than it should have; it may be that until I went off to college, I was still treating her with disdain, still refusing all offers to go to the park or the movies with her, still shouting at her to leave me alone when I was on the telephone.

Only when I returned to New York after the breakup of my first, brief marriage when I was twenty-four did my old love for her revive, along with the full realization of how sad her life had been. I went to see her once a week during that time; it was then that she told me sorrowfully, in a tremulous voice, about her beloved aunt dying in a mobile gas van and, though she was vague about details, the health troubles—something about his bowels—her father had suffered since his time in Dachau.

The worst story, though, the one that haunted me for a long time, was about the younger brother of a friend of hers, a man who, because he taught at a prep school in Connecticut, made a practice of picking up my sister and me in his car and driving us into New York on those weekends we spent with our mother. A shy, kind, slightly awkward man, who always made sure the car was warm enough for us, always brought along little snacks for us to eat during the drive, he was somebody we were fond of in an offhand sort of way, not a man we thought about much except when we were in his presence, but one we were always pleased to see.

What my mother told me was that, when he was a schoolboy in Fuerth in the late '30s, some of his classmates had trapped him in a corner of the schoolyard and castrated him with a kitchen knife. Not only that, but the teacher had stood by laughing. (I heard a similar story from a German woman who told of a nine-year-old Jewish girl in her class whom the teacher had thrown to the ground and encouraged the other girls to stomp on; those who held back were accused by the teacher of being Jew-lovers and traitors to the Führer. And so this woman, too, had entered in, though, she said, "I loved that girl very much." By the time they had finished, the child was dead.)

In 1973, my father was diagnosed with bone cancer. I visited my mother to break the news to her, and she covered her face with her hands, shaking her head silently, Oh no, no. Over the next sixteen months, I would bring her reports of the treatments he was receiving. First, they had amputated his leg at the knee, claiming that they had caught all the cancer, but just a month later they found cancer in the stump. In 1974, he was given various forms of radiation and chemotherapy, some of them new versions that were highly touted by the doctors, but none ever proved effective. Every time I had to tell my mother that the latest treatment had failed, she would collapse into her chair in sorrow. "That poor man," she'd murmur, "that poor man."

Finally the time came that they had run out of treatments to offer him, it was clear he was going to die. I went to break the news to my mother in person. She had tears running down her face, the only time I ever remember seeing her cry. "He used to write to me sometimes, you know," she said with timid pride. (Later I would see some of those letters, all typed by his secretary, with her initials at the bottom; the note of condolence that he'd written to her when my grandmother died said, "It is unfortunate that she was never able to establish with you the same warm relationship you have with your own daughters"—not mentioning that they were his daughters, too. I found it a chilly note, but apparently she did not.)

When, not long afterward, he died a painful death, she asked with the same timidity if she could go to his funeral in Connecticut. A girlfriend of mine, who'd visited her with me several times and grown fond of her, took her on the train, since I couldn't: I would be staying in the house with my stepmother and brother and sister the night before the ceremony. And so, in the room outside the sanctuary, my mother stood there in her baggy coat, a few feet away from my stepmother, who was flinging her arms around the dozens of mourners standing in line to talk to her. My mother could not have been more excluded; nobody except some relatives knew who she was, nobody talked to her except my friend; she had such a stricken look on her face that I could hardly bear it. I wished she hadn't come, for her sake. This was his life, these were the people, she had never known, all those well-dressed mourners lining up to console my stepmother, while my mother stood there unconsoled, and I looked on in frozen silence. It is a scene I wish I could erase from my memory.

Later that year, though, her life took a turn for the better: my sister and her husband had moved to Toronto, and my sister decided my mother should live there, too. For a while, they lived in the same apartment building; almost every day, my sister would bring her newborn son, her first child, upstairs to my mother's apartment, and they would play with him, or take him to the park if the weather permitted. When I phoned my mother in the first month she was there, she, who had never once told me she was unhappy, said, "This is the first time I've been happy in twenty-six years."

Then my sister became pregnant again, and they wanted a house of their own, so my mother bought one for them across town, with the money she'd inherited from my grandmother. She also bought them a car: my brother-in-law was not working full-time, or much at all, as he was studying for his accountancy exams, and my sister had not yet returned to teaching, having two small sons to look after. My mother was their chief source of funds. But she didn't seem to mind; she adored her grandchildren; she could hardly stop blowing kisses at them across the table.

Two years later, my brother-in-law failed his accountancy exams, and although he got various jobs in the insurance business, their financial position remained shaky. My sister went back to teaching, but sometimes she had to come and ask my mother for grocery money, which my mother never failed to provide. Though she always seemed reluctant to spend money on herself, even furnishing her apartment in Toronto with the same green armchair and green couch and pine desk that she'd had in New York—perhaps living through the inflation and depression of post-war Germany had left her frightened of being left destitute; perhaps the desk had been part of the furnishings of the apartment she'd shared with my father—she was extravagantly generous to the rest of us.

The only disapproval she ever expressed was about my sister becoming a practicing Jew. Not only had my mother never had any religious education herself—when she first went to school, and they asked what religion she practiced, she had to phone her father and ask—but she saw all religion as a force for ill, the cause of most of the wars and misery in the world. (Steven Runciman's scholarly denunciation of the Crusades as a barbaric invasion rather than a noble campaign to bring Christ to the heathen she regarded as one of the greatest historical works ever.) But perhaps Judaism was her least favorite religion: "At least the Catholic mass is short, and they don't have all those tiresome sermons." And she was sad that her grandchildren would not be allowed to celebrate Christmas: "Such a beautiful holiday." She deeply regretted the lack of a tree in their house, and having to present them with Chanukah presents, as she thought Chanukah a very poor substitute for Christmas. Later, at one of her grandsons' Bar Mitzvahs, she leaned over and whispered to me, "If this were television, I would turn it off."

A few years after her move to Canada, I got married again—to an Englishman, which should have pleased her, but she must have been shocked when I brought him to meet her, though she gave no sign of it: he had a beard down to his chest in those days, and looked like a wild man from the mountains, not at all the elegant male she might have hoped for—nor the head of a graduate program in fine art, which is what he was. Over the years, though, they became very good friends. They had long conversations on the phone about current events—deploring, for example, the pollution of the oceans and Ronald Reagan's support for the murderous right-wing regimes of El Salvador and

EVELYN TOYNTON

Guatemala. My husband would send her damning articles on the political situation from the *New York Review of Books*, and they took a sort of zestful pleasure in lamenting the nature of *Homo sapiens*, which they cheerfully agreed was unreconstructible. "How much nicer things will be," my mother would say, "when we've all killed each other off, or poisoned each other to extinction, and the animals can have the planet to themselves again." I used to offer to make them signs reading "The end of the world is at hand" they could march with through the streets.

After I had been married for several years—my mother had bought us a house, too, in Vermont—she asked me once, shyly, on one of my visits to Toronto, if I had ever told my husband about her brain operation. Amazed that she could possibly think I wouldn't have, I said, "Of course. And do you know what he said?" She shook her head. "He said, 'They could take away nine-tenths of your mother's brain, and she'd still be a lot smarter than most people.'"

"Oh," she said, "it's not true, but what a lovely thing to say." And the next week, when I phoned her, she told me, "I always used to go around with my head down, not talking to anyone; now I'm suddenly talking to everyone, I even get into conversations with people in the vegetable department at the supermarket." I am sure it was my husband's comment that gave her that confidence. Whatever troubles we would go on to have in our marriage, I could never stop being grateful to him for what that one remark had done for her. Even when we were separated for a while, and he was

42

back in England, he always stayed in touch with her, sending letters and postcards and phoning her on her birthday. (To spare her distress, we were both pretending that he was only in England to look after his own ailing mother.)

My mother was not free of medical problems in her new life. At one point, she started having fierce headaches again, and because they told her she might have a recurrence of the brain tumor, she gave my brother-in-law power of attorney over her assets. In the end, it turned out that there was no new tumor, it was the plate they had put in her brain that had slipped a little, but by then my brother-in-law had sold all the high-interest-bearing bonds my grandmother had left her and invested in a half-completed apartment in a new building complex, which he planned to resell at a profit. He had taken my husband and me to see it the last time we were in Toronto together, and my husband, who knew more about such things than I did, was alarmed at how jerry-built it seemed; the whole place looked flimsy to him, and he thought my brother-in-law had paid too much for it. But as he was an artist, and my brother-in-law a businessman, he brushed my husband's doubts aside.

Later, my mother began to have stomach troubles, ulcers were diagnosed, and finally, two years after my brother-in-law's purchase of the apartment, she told me that she would have to start asking my husband and me to pay her interest on the money she'd given us for the house; her only income came from a small pension from the company my father had headed up for years and the small portion of his social security that was due to her for their ten years of marriage. Meanwhile the apartment was still unsold; perhaps my brother-in-law was waiting for the price to increase. "Then why don't you just sell it for whatever you can get?" I asked her. "If you don't want to tell him [meaning my brother-in-law], I'll do it. I'll phone him right now and say you're selling it. And I'll get it listed with a real estate agent for you, you won't have to do anything."

"I can't sell it," she said miserably. "I can't."

"Why not?"

"Because it's in his name."

It seemed that my brother-in-law, maybe thinking that if my mother's brain tumor had returned, and proved fatal, it would eliminate any tax problems, had used his power of attorney to transfer my mother's assets into his name. When I heard that, I was furious; I got on the phone to my sister, who knew nothing about it, and made noises about suing him. Finally, after I'd hired a lawyer to write a threatening letter, he transferred the apartment back into my mother's name, and we got it sold, though she lost quite a bit of money on it. She would never again have high-yield bonds that she could count on for a comfortable income, but what was left of her inheritance after she'd bought those two houses and the car provided her with just enough money to live on in her modest way.

My husband had always been angry with my brother-in-law for not driving my mother, in the car she'd bought him, back to her own apartment, even in winter, after she came for dinner at the house she'd bought him. On nights when my sister was too busy with the children to serve as chauffeur, my mother, shaky as her balance was, had to walk from their house to the subway and then get on a train and walk back to her apartment on more streets covered with ice. But after the business with the apartment, my brother-in-law was less friendly than ever; as my mother said sadly, "Once someone has wronged you, they can never forgive you for it; you're just a reminder to them; they wish they didn't have to see you anymore."

Finally, on one of those icy pavements, she fell and broke her hip, and with her usual luck with doctors, the surgeon who performed the operation botched the job. (She used to say that her great hero was Mad King Ludwig of Bavaria, because when he drowned himself, he pulled his doctor down into the water with him.) At first, when she complained of excruciating pain, the surgeon accused her of malingering; nobody took her seriously until I got a doctor friend to phone the surgeon, pretending to be a cousin, and insist that the hip be X-rayed. ("Even for a surgeon," my friend said, "who aren't exactly known for their warmth, he was one cold son-of-a-bitch.") And when they did, they found that the hip had indeed been inserted wrong, which meant they had to open her up and operate again.

It took her a long time to recover, and in some sense she never did. More and more, she was losing her balance; my sister finally told her she was tired of coming over to her apartment to pick her up off the floor, and insisted that she go into a home. So I went to Toronto and we made the rounds of nursing homes together. Some of them reminded her of the place on Long Island where she had been sequestered forty years before; one was just a house where a woman took in elderly people and made meals for them. "Forget that one," I said as we left. And she said wryly, "After all, I haven't had such a very pleasant life; I think we have to find something a little nicer."

We did find something quite a lot nicer, and she moved in, but after a while my sister started getting phone calls from the manager, telling her that my mother, who during the years after the fiasco with my brother-in-law had taken to buying her clothes at the Salvation Army, was lowering the standards of the place. The other residents, this woman said, were complaining about her; she simply didn't fit in. I went to Toronto, where my sister and I went on a frantic search through all the clothes in my mother's closet and chest of drawers, getting rid of anything we felt could be seen as objectionable, and then shopped for new, more genteel-looking garments for her. But the manager was still not satisfied. Now she said my mother was too disabled to be there; because she had only one good hand, and could not use a knife and fork together, she had to resort to a scissors to cut her food into bite-sized pieces with her good hand. This, apparently, upset the other people at her table in the dining room. Also, because she had to dress herself using only one hand, her clothes, even the new ones, never seemed to hang properly; they always looked lopsided, as though listing to the left.

My husband argued with the manager, telling her how educated my mother was, how much she knew about politics and English history, how many languages she was fluent in—French, German, English—but the woman was unimpressed; she wanted my mother out of there as soon as possible.

So we found her another home, one where there were other residents with disabilities, and physiotherapy was offered, not that it did my mother much good. Still, she seemed content there at first; she made a friend—a pretty little widow whose room was adorned with dozens of dolls in frilly dresses—and the bookmobile came round once a week.

But her condition was deteriorating; whether it was the disc that had slipped in her brain or just the degeneration of old age, she soon had trouble seeing even with her good eye; she had to use a magnifying glass to read, while watching television became impossible; all the images on the screen blurred so much that she couldn't tell what was going on. Her gait, too, was getting worse; her legs wobbled under her; her ulcers had not quietened down completely after she got her money back, and she was racked with arthritis, even in her crippled arm. For the first time, she admitted to being miserable.

Then she got pneumonia, and we were told that she might not survive. I flew to Toronto, where she lay unconscious in the hospital, and when the doctor came to her bedside, assuring me that strong antibiotics might revive her, I asked him not to give them to her. She wouldn't want that, I said; I was sure she would prefer to die. But he, maybe thinking I was greedy for an inheritance, ignored that, and the strong antibiotics were injected into her veins. Once she regained consciousness, he told her, as though by way of a warning, that her own daughter had asked them not to revive her. "I wish you'd listened to her," she said. "I wish you'd let me go."

Shortly afterward, she had to be moved to yet another home; by that time she could barely see at all; she could not walk without holding on to someone's arm. When I visited her there, I was greeted with the sight of rows of silent old men and women—mostly women—slumped in wheelchairs in the lobby. Every time I walked in, I'd wonder what they would do if I went up to them and offered to kill them. I was sure that most of them would say Yes.

As her condition worsened, she was moved to the top floor, where the hopeless cases were, and had to keep the door to her room open so that the nurses and attendants could come and go freely. Most of the other residents on that ward were demented, as she decidedly was not; the ambulatory ones used to burst into her room and snatch her blanket, or accuse her of stealing things from them, or just rant at her about God and the devil until one of the attendants heard the shouts and came and led the intruder away.

Six months after her eighty-fifth birthday, she decided that such a life was not worth living; she asked my sister and me if we would help her find a way to die. At first I said I'd do it if my sister would. My plan was for both of us to get hold of barbiturates, still being prescribed then, by visiting our doctors and complaining of persistent insomnia. My sister, however, being religious, refused to be party to a suicide.

Then I, too, began to have doubts: I read Raymond Moody's *Life After Life*, about people who'd had near-death experiences and been revived. Those who had died accidentally reported being drawn toward a shining white light and feeling bliss such as they'd never experienced before. But those who had tried to kill themselves and been resuscitated had a whole different story to tell, of darkness rather than light: "These experiences were uniformly characterized as being unpleasant." Moody goes on to say, "Aquinas argues that life is a gift from God and that it is God's prerogative, not man's, to take it back."

Horrified, I told my mother that I was afraid for her; I couldn't bear to think of her suffering more pain in the afterlife when she'd already gone through so much of it on earth. "Maybe God really does punish people who refuse the gift of life," I told her. "Maybe there's something to what all those religions believe."

"If God wants me to go on living," she said tartly, "he ought to make my life a lot more pleasant than it is."

So, half thinking it was all just theoretical, but feeling I owed it to her to look into the matter, I bought a copy of *Final Exit*, the Bible of aspiring suicides. It seemed that even if she got hold of enough pills for the purpose, she would need to be able to tie a plastic bag over her head to ensure that she would die. With one arm crippled, and her other hand rendered almost as useless by arthritis, there was no chance she could do that.

And I was too squeamish, or not brave enough, to offer to tie the bag for her. Not only was the thought of doing it horrible in itself, in those days there were strict laws in Canada about helping people to die (the laws have since become slightly more flexible on the subject). I could not face being tried as an accessory to an illegal death, virtually a murderer. But a few months later an ex-student of my husband killed himself by swallowing a whole bottle of antihistamines, without tying a plastic bag over his head. They weren't even a prescription medicine; nobody could trace them back to me. I bought an extra-large jar of them and delivered it to my mother without telling my sister, and we said a tearful good-bye to each other. Two days after my return to New York, she phoned and told me that she had swallowed every pill in the bottle, and all that had happened was that she'd slept better than she had in years. "You must have the constitution of an ox," I said, and we both laughed at the preposterousness of that idea.

Within weeks, she phoned again, to tell me that she had not given up; she had decided to starve herself to death.

"What is the point," she asked, "of my being alive like this, with no pleasure at all, spending what little money we have left, so that you and your sister get nothing? It makes no sense." (Oddly, her pension from the company my father had headed up expired when she was eighty-five; I don't know if that was his doing, if he hadn't expected her to live very long, given her medical problems, or if the company itself had decided that was as long as they were willing to pay her.) She announced her plan to the attending doctor, who happened to be my sister's doctor also, and he told her airily that she would never go through with it; other patients of his who had tried had given up and begun eating and drinking again, because the process was so painful. He did not, however, tell her he would have her force fed if she attempted it.

And so she went ahead; she began refusing all food and drink. Within a week, she was barely conscious. I went back to Toronto, and when I entered her room and greeted her, she said faintly, with delight in her voice, "That sounds like Evie." "Of course it's Evie," I said, and she told me I shouldn't have come all that way. Knowing she would be dead within days, she still didn't think she was worth a plane trip.

It was clear from the look on her face, as much as from what I'd been reading about death from starvation, that she was in agony. When I asked an attendant on the ward what they were giving her to alleviate the pain, I was told that Tylenol was being "administered" every four hours. The doctor had warned her how painful slow starvation was, but had also assured her that he would not take any active measures to prevent her from dying. So why only Tylenol? Was he afraid that if he prescribed intravenous morphine, she would turn into a junkie in the few days she had left to live? Was it possible my sister had told him that she did not approve, and so he was reluctant to cooperate too fully? Or was he withholding strong pain medicine because it would hasten her death, and then he could be considered an accessory? But I didn't care what his reasons were; I just wanted him to do something to dull the pain.

There was a phone next to her bed, and the doctor's number in her address book on the dresser. I dialed it, and was put through what felt like an exceptionally long series of recorded messages: If this, press 1; then press 3; then press 1 again; then press 4. With every button I had to press, I became more hysterical, my sense of helplessness fueling my panic, until I was swearing down the phone in a rage, screaming at the machine voice: "Fuck this shit . . . Will some fucking human being kindly pick up this fucking phone," etc. For as long as I could remember, my mother had objected to my use of such words: "I don't understand why a young lady with such a command of the English language should have to resort to that sort of filth." And there I was at her deathbed, shouting filth at the top of my lungs.

Finally, I got through not to the doctor himself but to his individual voice mail. I introduced myself and said, as politely as I could, "I don't understand why you won't give my mother stronger pain medication. You know what she's doing, you haven't tried to stop her; she's in acute pain, that much is obvious, just as you said she'd be, yet all she's getting is Tylenol every few hours. Won't you please prescribe something that might actually give her some kind of relief? And will you please do it today? Thank you." Then I hung up and said, "The fucking asshole."

And my mother, who had just been listening to the most egregious stream of foul language I'd ever uttered in her presence, opened her eyes very slightly for the first time since I'd been there and whispered, in a voice full of tenderness, with more than a hint of amusement, "I love you." It was the last thing she ever said to me, or to anybody.

It took her six more days to die, and by the following morning she had lost consciousness altogether. I watched her wither before my eyes, her skin turning yellow, her mouth puckered from dehydration; she was absolutely still, I might have thought she was dead already, except for the faint sound of her breathing. Still, I knew that hearing was said to be the last thing to go, so I kept talking to her. I told her, among other things, that she had been a wonderful mother, which was true. I told her I was going to write about her someday, which I did, in a novel I published many years later. I told her I couldn't believe that God would be so cruel as to punish her, though for years afterward I worried about that, wondering if she had been sucked into the darkness described by the suicides in *Life After Life*.

Nobody was in the room with her when she died; I'd had to go back to my job, and so had my sister. So I don't know what my mother's last moments were like. All I know is that not a day has gone by since her death when I haven't thought of her, grieved for her, felt huge gratitude to her. Another woman might have been embittered and angry, might have lamented her fate to us, told us to watch out, reminded us that our lives, too, could change in an instant, we could lose everything we cared about. She might have told us never to trust anyone, men most of all, and spat out condemnations of our father for abandoning her. Instead, she told us funny stories about their life together.

And I am convinced that if it had not been for her, I would be a lot crazier than I am. My life with my father and stepmother was not such as to guarantee my sanity. However much of that quality I possess, I owe to my brain-damaged, crippled, half-blind mother, a woman considered unfit to have custody of her children, cast aside as a worthless member of society, with no possible use to anyone. She was of more use to me than any other human being I have known.

CHAPTER TWO:
The Public and Private Man

In his eulogy at the funeral, the rabbi said two things that described my father perfectly: "There was a monumental quality to him," and "There was no man more public in his purposes nor more private in his feelings." Not until long after his death, and the tributes to his public philanthropy that followed, did I start to see him as anything but monumental, or discover what his private feelings had been. Right until the time he died, when I was twenty-six, he was the monument that loomed over my life, and while he was alive, I never lost my sense of being in some essential way his child.

When I was very young, that had meant a feeling of perfect safety, such as I would never have again: he would always take care of me, always protect me from potential harm. When I scraped my knee in a fall on the playground, he picked me up in his arms and carried me home and dabbed iodine gently on the cut. On Aunt Ray's weekends off, he dressed me and fed me breakfast and read me stories, and clapped appreciatively as I turned cartwheels in the living room. For years, when he came home from work, he gave my sister and me a bath every night while telling us an ongoing saga about Giuseppe Giampoppa, an opera singer with a huge Italian family who together went all over the world singing and eating and shaking hands with Toscanini. He took me shopping for a dress to wear as a flower girl at a cousin's wedding, and let me buy exactly the one I wanted, pink with impractical black velvet ribbons. (Years later, I saw the same tenderness in him when a four-year-old girl who'd come to the house with her parents insisted he play patty-cake with her, which he did with a great show of interest, following all her instructions with a solemn attentiveness that delighted her.)

But when I was older, I would fall into disgrace and become a criminal in his eyes. To be his child then would mean living in the shadow of his constant moral disapproval. And however much I rebelled, I never doubted that he was a higher, worthier being, not subject to the ugly feelings of rage and hate and shame that burned in me.

Once, when he was six, my younger brother, the son of my father and stepmother, stuck a pin in a light switch and blew the fuse; my father emerged from his bedroom to find out what had happened and stood looking at my brother in silence. "Hit me," my brother burst out, "why don't you hit me, just don't look at me like that." But my brother, like my sister, rarely had that terrifying look turned in his direction. From the autumn of 1958, it was almost my father's habitual expression with me.

That summer the family—father, stepmother, sister, brother, and I—had moved from the cramped apartment in upper Manhattan where I had lived all my life to Danbury, Connecticut, a decaying hat factory town to which the pencil company my father ran had relocated. In New York, I had been a star pupil in what was known as the IG (intellectually gifted) class at P.S. 98. The lessons being taught in the fifth grade at Beaver Brook School in Danbury—an institution the state inspectors had graded as below adequate—were the same as we'd had two years earlier in New York, so fairly soon I stopped paying attention. Shortly after the school year started, my father was summoned to the principal's office and informed that I never did my homework; that when asked, I claimed that I'd left it at home. To my father, the departure from truth was the really grave offense. "What I find most disturbing is not that you didn't do your assignments but that you told your teacher a pack of lies." He quoted to me a German proverb, first in the original and then in translation: "Who lies will steal, who steals will kill." I was ten years old.

He must have felt I'd moved on to the next phase, with the third perhaps not long in coming, when, at the age of thirteen, I was caught shoplifting at Macy's in New York. My friend Jeannie, my accomplice, was the child of two Upper West Side psychiatrists who took our theft as a sign of psychological disturbance and sent her to therapy. My father, however, saw it as further proof of my immoral nature, which made him despair of me; if I kept going like that, he said, I would wind up in jail before I was twenty-one.

And if that were to happen, he would have to think very carefully about whether to bail me out.

Shortly afterward, I swallowed a bottle of aspirin in a feeble suicide attempt and vomited for several hours; when the pediatrician was called in to treat me, I admitted to him what I had done. My father, like Jeannie's parents, then decided I needed psychiatric help, and sent me to a fancy child psychiatrist in Westport, who seemed to think he could form a bond with me by discussing literature. We spent practically a whole session arguing about whether Jews should refuse to read Dickens because of his anti-Semitism; he took the view that they should boycott any writer who showed that kind of prejudice, whereas I, a thirteen-year-old aesthete—I was in love with Oscar Wilde; I had a special notebook in which I copied out my favorites of his aphorisms—insisted that it was not a writer's opinions but the quality of his prose that mattered, though actually I wasn't very keen on Dickens.

My father took off work early once a week to drive me to my appointments, but he never asked me what had gone on during my sessions, or spoke much at all on the way to and from Westport. Perhaps he had to concentrate very hard on the road: having learned to drive only after the move to Connecticut, when he was almost fifty, he was a cautious but inept driver, often going up on curbs. Or maybe he was turning over important business affairs in his mind. Whatever the reason, the silence felt to me like a reproach: I imagined him thinking how humiliating, how undignified, it was that some stranger should be hearing the intimate details of our family life, all because he had a bad seed for a daughter.

After I had been seeing the shrink for a few months, my stepmother blurted out, when I had once again failed to put some soiled clothes in the hamper, "That Dr. Siegel said we have to be nice to you, but it's all very well for him. He doesn't know what a dirty person you are, how hard it is to be nice to someone like you." All in all, it was a failed experiment. And so, untherapized, I sank further into shame and rage and suburban juvenile delinquency. I played hooky—another summons to the principal's office; I phoned in a bomb scare to my high school; I cheated on my chemistry test and failed geometry. At fourteen I started sneaking cigarettes in the bathroom, something my older sister felt obliged to report to my father, because, she explained, she was worried about me. (My sister was so completely the good daughter and I so completely the bad one, we might have been characters in a fairy tale; the fact that we had a wicked stepmother—even my mild-mannered sister referred to her as "the witch"—made it two fairy tales in one.)

At one point my father decided that all his children should learn another language, and I was assigned to German. The German speaker he hired to give me private lessons happened to be the organist at my friend Pam's church, and I knew from her that his wife had just left him, and the congregation was concerned about his drinking. So when he began showing up at my weekly lessons smelling of liquor, I saw him as a tragic, romantic figure, of the kind I was always reading about in books (after all, Swinburne had been an alcoholic), and would have considered it traitorous to squeal on him to my father. Pretty soon Herr Lange was not only turning up drunk but falling asleep soon after the lesson started. That was very easy to forgive, since it meant I didn't have to do much preparation: I was supposed to be learning "Der Ring des Polykrates" by Schiller, but Herr Lange rarely stayed awake beyond the first verse.

As my father never tested me on my progress, and was never at home in the afternoons, when the lessons took place, he might have remained unaware of the situation indefinitely if the cleaning woman who came several times a week had not answered the door to Herr Lange one day and smelled liquor on his breath. She felt obliged to report the matter to my stepmother, who told my father, who interrogated me—though still without trying to determine how much German I'd actually learned—in a tone that made it clear he didn't share my sense of Herr Lange as a figure of romance. Poor Herr Lange was informed that his services were no longer required, and I was given a stern talking-to: Had it never occurred to me, my father asked, that while Herr Lange was driving to or from my lesson in that condition, he might have accidentally killed either himself or someone else?

But if my father was eternally displeased with me, in his somber, magisterial way—he never once raised his voice during those lectures in his den—I was seething with sullen rage toward him. I wanted him to understand that I was miserable, I wanted him to comfort instead of reproach me, to ask me what was wrong, which he never did. Nor did it occur to me to tell him outright; his grave and formal manner with me, more like that of a headmaster than a parent, made it unthinkable. Yet I felt he should have known without my having to say anything; most of all, I felt he should be defending me against my stepmother, our domestic commissar, who alternated more and more between snarling insults and menacing silences that might or might not erupt into slaps across the face or assaults with dishtowels.

Back in New York, my stepmother had seemed like a manageable nuisance, an obstacle to happiness that could be skirted around most of the time. I could go out and play with my friends in the neighborhood, I could visit my mother whenever I pleased. I was not yet regarded as a problem child, even if, shortly after my stepmother moved into the apartment in New York and Aunt Ray was banished, I had begun wetting the bed.

My stepmother was affronted by my bed-wetting, she being the one who had to change the sheets. When my fourth-grade teacher invited me to her apartment on a Sunday night, in order to read my poems to a group of her friends, my stepmother, stripping the bed that morning, had shouted at me that she was going to tell my teacher that "the little genius" pissed in her bed every night; maybe Mrs. Lewis wouldn't think I was such a goddamn genius then. (My stepmother wasn't much of a poetry lover, my own or anybody else's.)

During the year before we moved, she was often in Connecticut all day, overseeing the building and decoration of the new split-level house that she had decided she preferred to an old Colonial. So instead of my going back to the apartment for lunch, she would pack me a brown paper bag with two baloney sandwiches to take to school—I hated baloney, but she would not indulge my preferences; it was time, she said, that I learned to eat what I was given. Instead, I would walk to my mother's apartment during lunch hour, and we would eat cheese and crackers together and talk about Anne Boleyn. But I had stupidly failed to dispose of those packed lunches; I had hidden two, still in their brown bags, in the back of the closet in the bedroom I shared with my sister, and when my stepmother found them, she was furious.

Still, it was always my father who really counted in that household; as long as I felt sure of his love, my stepmother was just an irritating intrusion into my life; she couldn't really affect my sense of self. Despite the power she wielded, I'm afraid that even when very young, I saw her, with her shrill Brooklyn accent, the coarse language she habitually used, as unworthy of my father, which was also how she saw herself—no doubt a huge part of the problem. (My father seemed to show no such snobbery toward her. I think at the outset of their relationship, when presumably she was being more pleasant, he may have seen her accent and her language as simply American. And there must have been some sexual attraction that I had no sense of as a child.)

But after the move to Danbury, she could no longer be sidestepped; while my father worked longer and longer hours, we three children were trapped in the house with her. It had become her obsession to keep it completely spotless, which our very existence rendered impossible. However many times we wiped our feet, we brought traces of dirt into the house, or at least into the rooms we were permitted to enter; we slopped water in the bathroom, made smells, soiled the refrigerator door with our fingerprints every time we opened it, until, if we wanted an apple or a glass of milk, we had to ask her to get it for us, with a fifty-fifty chance she'd agree. Maybe, somewhere in her Catholic mind, she equated dirt with sin. Or maybe she simply felt we weren't grateful enough for her efforts, which she refused all help with, not trusting us to do anything properly. Whatever the reason, the phrase "dirty pig" was deployed a lot.

And my father, even when he was at home, was mostly downstairs in his den, working through the huge stacks of paper piled on his desk and seemingly oblivious to what was going on upstairs, where my stepmother reigned supreme. I could no longer go and visit my mother, my refuge, whenever I wanted; she was sixty miles away. I was trapped, hiding out in my room (due to my stepmother's paranoia, my sister and I weren't allowed in each other's bedrooms, though we managed to sneak little visits, mostly to exchange whispered complaints about the witch). But I never felt entirely safe; I never knew when my stepmother might burst in with some fresh accusation.

When he arrived back from the office, my father, in his gentlemanly way, would ask her polite questions about her day, trying to draw her out of her sulk, and she would shout at him that he didn't really care, he didn't give a shit about her day, or about her; nobody cared about her, why didn't he just cut the crap. I think she genuinely believed that; her bitterness was real, she saw herself as nothing but the skivvy, but as she would not allow anyone to help with her chores except the cleaning woman, it was impossible for her to be otherwise.

My father remained calm, stately, in the face of these assaults; he did not lose his dignity, but that wasn't what I wanted from him: I wanted him to shout back, to pound his fist on the table and order her to shut up, even to smack her face as she sometimes smacked mine. I was convinced that mere words would never have the desired effect; it was brute force that was called for. (In fact, I still think it might have worked.) I knew, though, that he would never resort to that.

Instead I fantasized about killing her. I imagined how happy the four of us could be with her dead, how we'd sit around the kitchen table talking about this and that, as we sometimes did when she was at Sunday mass, before scattering to our respective rooms when we heard her car in the drive. My favorite plan was to string a very fine plastic thread, invisible to the naked eye, across the top of the stairs, so that she'd tumble down and crack her head on the immaculately clean tiles below. But like my father, and despite the grim German proverb branding me as a killer for not doing my homework, I lacked the nerve.

Nor did I tell anyone else about this murderous fantasy, my father least of all. In fact, my sister had impressed on me that we were never to complain to my father about our stepmother, because it could only cause him distress. She also told my brother and me not to ask him any questions about Germany, because it might awaken painful memories for him. In retrospect, I'm not sure that was a sound piece of psychology, but at the time we thought she must understand these matters better than we did, and refrained from mentioning the few small reminders of his past the house contained.

So I never asked him about the tiny colored etching next to the front door, which showed a half-timbered building next to a river and an ancient-looking bridge, with church spires in the background. (Now I know that it was the fourteenth-century Nuremberg Weinstadel, originally built to house lepers and later turned into a wine storehouse.) I didn't even ask about my grandparents, whose stern, unsmiling photographs—perhaps they had been taken during the Nazi years—sat on my father's bedroom dresser for as long as I can remember.

Whatever I knew of these grandparents, or my father's life before he came to America, I learned from his elder brother, my Uncle Hans. My grandfather had been very lenient with his three sons when they were young, Hans said; he preferred playing and joking with them to disciplining them, so matters of discipline were left to their mother, which was not difficult to believe, since she looked even more severe than my grandfather in the photograph on my father's dresser. Hans also told me about my great-grandfather, a leading citizen of Nuremberg, a Geheimrat (King's counselor) to the Court of Bavaria, head of the Bavarian Bar Association, head of the Jewish community, widely regarded as a sage—when he died, the mayor of Nuremberg gave one of the eulogies at his funeral. "Although we three boys didn't really know our grandparents," Hans said, "we grew up in this legendary grandfather's shadow somehow. We didn't understand it, sometimes we resented it a little, but it was a fact."

Another thing my uncle told me was that when my father was twelve or thirteen, their mother had said she couldn't see what future there was for him; he didn't seem interested in anything but football, something I found impossible to imagine. But perhaps that's why, when my grandfather fell into a deep depression—his business had collapsed in the soaring inflation of 1920s Germany; he may also have been suffering from the aftermath of his service in World War I, during which he'd suffered the wound in one arm that left it virtually useless—it was my fourteen-year-old father, rather than his older brother, who was taken out of school and sent to work. Hans was the colorful, domineering one; Georg, the youngest, the shining intellectual light. My father was clearly more expendable; he could be sent to earn money, first as an office boy, then as a clerk, since he had no future anyway.

Years after my father's death, my brother sent me a photograph of the three brothers, all of them in short trousers and lace-up boots, taken when my father looked to be six or seven. It must have been during the First World War, when my grandfather was off serving in the German Army; perhaps their mother wanted him to see how much his sons had grown in his absence. Hans towers over my father, as he would all his life—my father was the runt of the family, his two brothers being well over six feet while he was a mere five-feet-ten—and is looking into the camera with supreme confidence; Georg, who would have been four or five, has the scowl of a child who has been dressed up for a photograph and just wants to go off and play. My father, meanwhile, looks shy and anxious, almost fearful. No one could have predicted, looking at that photograph, that he would one day be described as monumental.

In fact, Hans still seemed surprised that his brother had had a future after all. When my father was dying slowly of cancer, Hans said to me, not unkindly but musingly, "I never would have thought that Rolf would be so successful. We all assumed he wouldn't make much of his life." (He had started out in America as a clerk in the import-export department of the Eagle Pencil Company; he wound up the head of the firm, expanding it internationally until it was more than triple the size it had been when he was first hired, enriching the sons of the founder many times over without ever owning any shares in the company himself.) What my father thought of his career in America, I have no idea; certainly he never boasted about it, being almost pathologically modest.

But of all the brothers, in fact all my relatives, he was the first to emigrate, in January 1933—as my mother put it, for a German Jew, it was equivalent to having been on the *Mayflower*. He never talked about what he had seen, or what had happened to him, that made him leave even before Hitler became chancellor. But in 1923, a whole decade before anyone thought the Nazis would ever wind up in power—even in 1928, they had won only 3 percent of the vote in the national election—they had begun holding rallies in Nuremberg, which they regarded as their symbolic home. With its ancient fortifications, its medieval towers and bridges, it was the perfect place to act out their fantasy of themselves as the rightful heirs of the old Teutonic knights, and from 1927 on, all their rallies were held here. Under Julius Streicher, the zealous, violently anti-Semitic Gauleiter of Franconia, the party in the greater Nuremberg area became the best-organized branch in all Germany. When fledgling Brownshirts beat up my grandfather in the street in the late '20s, they were already acting with impunity; the Nuremberg police were known to be sympathetic to the Nazis.

So my father's reason for emigrating could not have been simply the lure of America that had drawn so many millions of Europeans before him. America was in the midst of the worst depression in its history; the myth of streets paved with gold had been exploded. But my grandfather was seeing the slow buildup, right in his birthplace, to what would become the greatest pogrom in history. He got in touch with some distant relatives in New York City, the owners of the pencil company, and once they'd agreed to interview my father, at least, for a job with their firm, the decision was made that he would go to America.

When I was in my final year of college, and the specter of my winding up in jail had receded, I once asked my father if he didn't feel strange returning to Germany, where he went on business several times: Did he not harbor some residual resentment toward the Germans he encountered? It was still the '60s, barely two decades after the end of the war; many of the people he dealt with in German companies could have served in the *Einsatzgruppen*, murdering Jews on the Eastern Front, or as guards in a concentration camp. But "No," he told me, "these people are not Nazis. Germany is an entirely different country now." It was a frustrating response, too mild and passionless to satisfy me. I couldn't understand why he felt no thirst for vengeance. (He didn't say, as he might have done, that it was more complicated for him, that he had loved his country when he was young, or that he had known many Germans who were nothing like the SS men singing lustily about Jewish blood dripping from their knives, cracking open the heads of Jewish babies.)

By the time we had the conversation about Germany, my father's disapproval of me had totally abated; in fact, he was more pleased with me than he'd been since I was a small child. This change was due not to anything I'd done, but to my having attracted a suitor he admired almost to the point of veneration: a graduate of Harvard and of Harvard Medical School. I suspect it seemed astonishing to my father, almost a miracle, that such a fine upstanding young man should want to marry his feckless daughter. (My fiancé was also fantastically rich, but I honestly don't think that played much part in my father's esteem for him. It was Harvard, above all, that did it. Having left school at fourteen himself, my father had a wildly exaggerated notion of what an American college degree entailed. While he had learned both Latin and Greek at the *Gymnasium* in Nuremberg, and spoke fluent Spanish as well as English and German, he assumed that even someone with a BA from the local teacher's college would be more educated than he was. Imagine how impressive two degrees from Harvard seemed to him.)

I was not so enthusiastic about the young man as he was, but every time I decided to break off my engagement, every time I returned to Connecticut and announced that I wasn't getting married after all, my father would sit me down in his den and urge me to think the matter over carefully: "Not that I wish to influence your decision in any way [a characteristic phrase of his], but Michael seems like such a fine person, I can't help wondering if you aren't making a terrible mistake you'll regret later." And so I would go back, not because I thought my father was right but because I wanted so much to please him; I was afraid that he would never forgive me if I didn't marry this man.

Two years into the marriage, my father phoned me and told me that they had found cancer in his bones. When my husband got back from his session with his psychoanalyst that day and found me crying about this news, he paced angrily up and down for a few minutes before saying, "I know you expect me to sympathize with you, but when I was a child, my mother always demanded sympathy from me, and I really resented it." Despite the clear evidence of my grief at my father's news, he also repeatedly accused me of hating my father so much that I could never really love anybody. After a few months during which I slept very little and wondered if maybe I was really as full of hatred as my husband said, I decided that I could not bear the siege any longer, the constant psychoanalyzing of my character defects, and moved out.

One week later, my father and I had our last stormy confrontation, in what would be the first of his many hospital rooms—the beginning, when I look back on it, of our final reconciliation. It was about my refusal to ask my husband for any of his family's millions in the divorce. Fortunately, by that time, my father's opinion of my husband was not so high, Harvard or no; he was no longer upset that I was ending the marriage, only that I wasn't demanding any money. And he was furious that my husband wasn't offering me any.

He must have known then, or at least suspected, that he was going to die—it was after the doctors had amputated his leg at the knee, to stop the cancer from spreading, and then discovered more cancer in the stump. He must have worried about what would happen to his impractical daughter, who had no seeming ambition to do anything in particular, who had never had a job, only two useless degrees in English literature, with a thesis on Coleridge that would not guarantee her remunerative employment. He was going to hire an *amicus curiae*, he told me, a friend of the court, to represent me in the divorce. (I hadn't even hired a lawyer; I was allowing my husband to sue me for desertion without any protest from me.) But I was in my loftiest mode, full of a sense of my own nobility: now I was the morally pure one, refusing to take money I hadn't in any way earned. So I told him, sitting up straight in the chair by his bed, that if he did that, I would never speak to him again.

A minute later, though, I burst into tears. "You've been poor," I wailed. "Why shouldn't I be poor?" He gave me a startled look: he had never mentioned the poverty of his early years; it was something I knew of only from my mother and my uncle, but I think he understood my point—I wanted a chance to prove myself, too; I didn't want some man supporting me all my life. Or maybe he was touched that I would even care about his having been poor. Whatever the reason, he never brought up the subject of a settlement again; the divorce went through uncontested. Sometime later, my soon-to-be-ex-husband wrote my father an unctuous letter, saying how sorry he was that the marriage had not worked out, how much he would miss seeing him and my stepmother—a blatant untruth. My father responded in a curt, uncharacteristically rude note, the carbon of which I found in his desk after his death; I only wish I had kept it. Its last line was, "I'll thank you never to trouble me again."

But what of those public purposes of which the rabbi spoke in his eulogy? They had all been philanthropic, practically since his arrival in America. While working at his job all day, my father had spent his evenings and weekends in the '30s working with refugee committees engaged in finding sponsors for German Jews hoping to come to America; if would-be immigrants had no relatives prepared to vouch for them, the committee would make appeals to prosperous members of the German Jewish community in New York. Some of the city's affluent Jews were distant relatives of my father, and shared his surname, which perhaps was helpful when he had to approach them: second cousins of his had established a brokerage house in the early 1900s that had made them very rich by the '30s, despite the economic slump.

As he grew more prosperous over the years, my father gave generously to many charities, more and more so as his salary increased. But he also put in a lot of work on the causes important to him. He spearheaded a referendum to raise taxes for the overhaul of Danbury's school system, until it passed all its state inspections. For nearly a decade, he served on the board of trustees for the local hospital, chairing the long-range planning committee, establishing links with the hospitals at Yale. When he was not going over the mounds of paper that he brought home every night, relating to the pencil company, he was formulating plans for the hospital's expansion, or out at meetings of the hospital board. All that, I'm afraid, I'd resented too: there he was, busy making the world a better place for strangers, while back in his house his three children were being bullied and shouted at, accused of various heinous infractions by an unappeasable stepmother. (As my brother grew up, she increasingly became an equal opportunity abuser, as hostile to him as she was to my sister and me.)

Another of my father's philanthropic initiatives, surely related to his own experience of going into debt to pay for my mother's brain surgery, was to provide health insurance for all employees in the company's South American branches, the first time a corporation had ever done that. For that reason there is, or at least was, a portrait of him hanging in the National Capitol in Bogotá, Colombia. He also attempted, very early on in the Civil Rights Movement, to hire and train more Blacks to work in the American operations. And when he was appointed to the governor's commission on drugs, he became one of the few members in favor of legalizing marijuana.

As for those private feelings the rabbi mentioned: I know of only one occasion when he revealed any raw emotion. It was after my stepmother had been particularly vicious to him, to all of us, for days on end. My sister, with whom my stepmother accused him of being in love, found him sitting in his den with his head in his hands; looking up at her, he said, "She's God's judgment on me for what I did to your mother." I wasn't there, I didn't see his face as he spoke; I can only imagine what a wrench it must have been for him to let those words escape his mouth.

I have sometimes wondered if I reminded him of my mother as I was growing up, if that was painful for him. My sister was so clearly his daughter, hardworking and steadfast and responsible, whereas I was my mother's, not in what he deemed my criminality but in my carelessness about practical matters, my frivolous love of clothes and girly things, my voracious novel reading. ("I can't understand," he once said with genuine bewilderment, "why anybody would want to read made-up stories, when there's so much of interest to be learned about real people and events.") He certainly knew that I was much

75

closer to her than to him, that she had imbued me with her romantic Anglophilia.

A month before he died, when I was alone with him in his hospital room, my father asked me, for the first time that I could remember, how my mother was. I did not tell him that she had cried when she heard he was dying; maybe I didn't feel he deserved to know that. I only said she was fine, and left it at that. And he didn't pursue it. Too much had been left unsaid for too long to make it possible for us to talk about my mother to each other.

One of the last times I was alone with him in the hospital—my uncle and my stepmother had gone to the cafeteria to get something to eat—he came as close as he ever would to apologizing to me for what my stepmother had put me through. By then all the measures that had been taken to halt the spread of his cancer—not just the amputation but the several bouts of radiation and chemotherapy the doctors had expressed such hope for—had proved futile. He had accepted that he would die very soon, and spoke of his death with perfect calm, though only briefly, being more inclined to discuss impersonal things: the Watergate crisis, a disturbing piece in the *New York Times* about elderly women living on cat food because they could not afford anything else. But once the others had left the room that day, he stopped talking about that morning's newspaper. For a moment he fell silent; he cleared his throat, he took a deep breath, not easy for him by then, and told me, looking steadily at my face, that he had asked my stepmother over and over through the years to go to marriage counseling with him. "But she always refused; even when I begged her, she wouldn't do it."

It was a plea for understanding, the first time he had acknowledged, if only indirectly, how awful things had been in that house: he was telling me that he had at least tried to make them better. I should have given him absolution then, said it wasn't his fault, there was nothing more he could have done. But I couldn't so easily erase my resentment at all those years of petty tyranny, those onslaughts he'd failed to protect me from; even when he was dying, I couldn't summon that kind of generosity, though it was my last chance. I brushed him off with some callow remark about how, oh well, they had been such different kinds of people, she was so much more upfront with her emotions, that was the problem. And he did not pursue the subject any further. He knew, I think, that what I was really saying was that I did not forgive him.

And yet I grieved for him all the time he was dying. I grieved for the pain he was suffering in those last weeks, as the doctors withdrew, as the cancer moved in for the kill; when his door was ajar once, I saw him gripping the railings of the bed, his head thrown back, his teeth clenched in agony, although once I'd knocked and entered, he folded his hands on his chest and arranged his face in a smile. After that I prayed that he could die quickly, to escape from his suffering; I saw that to be freed of his pain would be heaven enough. He didn't die that week, or the next—dying seemed as hard as being born—but throughout that time I thought all I wanted was for him to die, I was willing it to happen for his sake.

Yet when it finally happened, I spiraled into a state of pure terror, surrounded by a huge hollow space that seemed to pulse with his absence. Every night, I lay on my bed, pushing my mind further into that void, trying to follow him there, to reach its end point, which was eternity: that was how long he would be dead, the never my brain could not encompass was when I would see him again. Riding the subway, I would stare in horror at some weasel-faced boy in a dirty jacket reading a porn magazine: *Why should a dog, a horse, a rat have life, and thou no breath at all?*

And my grief brought me face-to-face with a crazy hope that must have lain buried in me for twenty years at some hidden, unconscious level, below reason and thought: that someday my mother and father would be reunited, we would be the family that had been destroyed by the surgeon's bungled operation and my father's inability to love who my mother became afterward. Now I had to confront the knowledge that it could never happen, a truth as hard to bear as his death itself.

After weeks of barely sleeping, I phoned my sister in Canada, sobbing, and asked her to tell me her recollections of our parents, she having been three when everything fell apart. One of her happiest memories, she said, was of them all taking showers together, something I could hardly believe of my very correct father, whose chest, whose legs, I had never seen; they were always covered. When we hung up, I finally fell into a deep sleep, to dream of my parents smiling at each other on the deck of a ship, my mother in a beautiful pale straw hat and shoes with ankle straps, my father in a linen suit. Though I woke up in tears, and my mind started in again on its frantic attempt to follow never into infinity, for a whole minute I believed that it was a real memory: I had traveled back in time and seen them as they'd once been.

Weeks later, my brother sent me a copy of something he had found in my father's desk, the carbon of a long letter my father had written to my stepmother thirteen years before, when he was leaving on a two-month-long business trip. I can only think that he meant it to be found, since he had cleared out so many of his other papers: he must have wanted his children to read it, to know that once he had prayed to die, for his plane to crash, so that he wouldn't have to return to that house in Danbury.

He had come back to have lunch with my stepmother before he left on his trip, he wrote, only to find that she hadn't bothered to get dressed, hadn't prepared any lunch for him, that "your farewell to me was an argument about what I was going to take out of the ice box. Why could you not just let me go in peace? Why did you have to show me even on that last day that I meant less than nothing to you? I have had to carry that as a heavy burden around the world with me."

He'd found himself praying, he said, that he wouldn't have to come back, that his plane would fall into the ocean. "As I come nearer the end of this journey, I become even more panicky and wonder over and over: do I have to go back to Danbury? If so, do I have to live in Country Ridge or should I simply move into a hotel or a room? If I go to Country Ridge, would it be better for me to move down into the den and avoid contact with you as much as possible?

"I fear the unbridled tongue, the cutting, biting remarks that hurt, the belittling of everyone, the tendency to question motives, the constant carping criticism. I fear the furious answer to innocent questions or innocent requests by the children, like asking to be picked up from a rehearsal. I fear the hurricane that comes over the horizon and lashes everything in sight, the thunderstorm that does so much violence and damage.

"Ten years from now the nameless creatures—my two daughters have hardly ever been called anything but 'the dolls' or the 'big doll' or 'the little doll,' with the inflection in your voice that shows the depth of your dislike, I almost called it hatred—might be married or might have children. To make sure that this would not do too much for my happiness, I have had advance notice that you will not be interested in their offspring. In fact, you once told me that if you never saw either of them again, you would not care."

It went on like that for four single-spaced typed pages. But he did return to the house at the end of that trip, maybe for the sake of his children, though if he had moved out permanently, my sister and I would have lived with him, and been glad of our escape. But my brother would almost certainly have been left alone with his mother, a woman even more bitter and angry than she had been up till then. So he still feels nothing but gratitude to my father for sticking it out.

Once he was ill, though, my stepmother ceased her tantrums completely; she visited him in the hospital every day, incessantly cracking the sort of jokes that before had been reserved for when outsiders were present. ("Hi, honey, I've brought you your mail—I bet you'd prefer a female, huh?") In fact, I wished she were not always so insistently in attendance; I was always waiting for my moments alone with him, when she was at the hairdresser's or downstairs grabbing something to eat, even if our conversations then, with a few exceptions, were as formal and impersonal as ever.

Still, my stepmother's devotion was absolute, not to be doubted; it was as if she had been waiting all those years for a chance to be of service to him—to show him, as she could not throughout their marriage, that she loved him, which strangely enough I believe she did. She became fiercely protective, quick to note any sign of neglect on the part of a nurse or orderly, which of course he would never complain of himself, even if he were left in sweat-soaked pajamas for hours. But her greatest ire—"I could spit in their faces"—was directed toward those who failed to visit him, among whom were several up-and-coming younger men he had mentored at the office, and the owners of the company, whom he had enriched a hundredfold while they raised horses in Bedford Hills and got sued by showgirls for breach of promise. (I once asked him if he didn't think it was unfair that he should do all the work while they got all the profits. "Not at all," he said. "Their father gave me my first job when I came to America.")

In one of our last moments alone, before he started drifting in and out of consciousness, he asked me to promise I'd go on seeing my stepmother after his death, because "otherwise all the burden will fall on Richie." I could not very well refuse, though when I escaped from the house in Danbury on the day of his funeral—my stepmother had been cursing out my brother a minute before we left for the synagogue, because his shoes were unpolished—I didn't see how I could stand ever to speak to her again. It was she who made the first move: she phoned me at my apartment in the city and asked to come see me.

Once she'd arrived, I realized that on the mantelpiece, in her direct line of sight, was the carved ivory statue I had removed from my father's den after his funeral without asking permission, and I waited for an explosion of wrath. It was almost like a showdown in a Western, our eyes fixed on each other, waiting to see who would blink first. And she was the one who looked away; not a word was said about the ivory figure above the fireplace. She knew, I think, that she couldn't risk an attack, her power over me was gone—I could shout at her in return if I wanted, tell her to get out and never come back.

For a while that only made me angrier with her: for all those years I had seen her as out of control, unable to stop herself from those furious outbursts. Now she'd shown that she was perfectly able to restrain herself when necessary. Which meant that giving vent to all her ugliest feelings had been a form of self-indulgence; she had not bothered to stop herself, knowing there would be no real consequences.

When, decades later, I came to read about narcissistic personality disorder, it was uncanny how many symptoms she'd had: "Requires constant, excessive admiration and gratitude . . . has an inability or unwillingness to recognize the needs and feelings of others . . . easily feels slighted . . . uses contempt as a weapon and tries to belittle the other person . . . has secret feelings of insecurity and humiliation . . . expects unquestioning compliance . . . flies into a rage when their need for affirmation is not met to the degree they require."

But from the day she came to my apartment, she was nothing but civil to both me and my sister; she was generous, too, sending us money for our birthdays and at Christmas, keeping in touch with us at regular intervals for the forty years she outlived my father. She even left us money in her will.

One Saturday when she phoned, a year after my father's death, she asked me what I was doing, and I told her nothing much; I was only half watching the film *Mommie Dearest* on television. "I bet that Crawford bitch doesn't seem too bad, huh, after what I did to you," she said. Another time, she told me she realized how much her own childhood had screwed her up: one of thirteen children, with all her parents' devotion lavished on their sons rather than their daughters, she had always felt, she said, "like a worthless piece of shit."

So it was no longer simple to go on hating her, though I could never love her either. There was no pleasure for me in any of those calls or, even worse, the visits to Connecticut. I had to grit my teeth as I listened to her gabbling on, and sooner or later, every time, the old, murderous rage rose in me again. Especially if there was someone else present, and she was sighing about her "dear husband"—she even said once how he'd loved to take her dancing, a ridiculous notion—I felt a churning in my stomach, the taste of bile in my throat. But at least I had kept my promise to my father. I had failed him so many times, in so many ways, when he was alive, just as he had failed me, but in that one thing, after his death, I came through.

CHAPTER THREE: *The Exile*

In his physical presence, at least, my father's elder brother was a perfect specimen of the old-fashioned patriarch. Larger, louder, fiercer than anybody else, he dominated every family gathering, his laughter as thunderous as his rage, and both somehow unmistakably German in cadence. To show up ten minutes late, to oppose the most minor of his dictates, was to witness what looked like the beginnings of apoplexy. Sometimes his meekly adoring wife would clutch at my arm and plead with me to leave, afraid he might burst a blood vessel if he kept shouting at me. (My mother, when I returned to her apartment after one of those explosions, would shake her head and say indulgently, "The problem with you and Hans is that you're too much alike." The very idea made me indignant: How could she possibly even think such a thing? Was she really comparing me to that horrible man? It didn't occur to me at the time that, glaring and shouting as I was, I was actually confirming her point.)

But imperious though he was, my uncle was hardly a patriarch in the grand moral sense. While others in the family devoted themselves to good works, he seemed to take no interest in serious causes. At the age of fifty, claiming that his two brothers worked hard enough for three, he had quit his hated job in a brokerage house to lead his idea of the good life, dragging his complaisant wife to the Serengeti Plain and across the Indian subcontinent, taking up residence in Europe every summer. He spent a month at an archaeological site in Greece and got a visa to visit the pyramids by claiming, on his application, to be a Catholic rather than a Jew. When in New York, he appeared to spend most of his time in restaurants, although he frequented museums also, and occasionally auction houses, buying himself two unsigned Renaissance portraits of Italianate-looking men, with verdant hills and tiny crooked houses in the background. These he hung in the shabby one-bedroom apartment in Inwood he'd moved to when he and his wife first arrived in New York, and which he saw no need to desert when affluence was upon them.

He entertained himself in odder ways, too—taking private lessons in Finnish, for example, and in Hungarian, because he found it droll to compare the differences among languages; busying himself with the immigration problems of the waiters in his favorite restaurants. He would spend the afternoon, after the lunch crowd had gone, with their naturalization forms spread out on the table before him, talking to them in his pidgin Greek or Italian or Hindi—booming with laughter, insisting that they correct his mistakes; like many lonely people, he always seemed most at ease with strangers. Sometimes he sent one of them to his lawyer for help with a green card, just as he had sent the cleaning lady in his office to California for a vacation. For his generosity was as immoderate as his wrath.

But while my father's philanthropy tended to consist of serving on committees to improve the state of things, Hans's was always focused on the individual. (It was he who told my sister and me about the fate of what had happened to the husband and sons of my grandmother's friend Emmy at the hands of the Nazis; it was coming up to Emmy's seventy-fifth birthday, for which he would be sending her flowers, and though we had barely ever met her, he wanted us to write her a card, because there were so few people who would know or care that it was her birthday.)

At one point, he decided that my mother needed a television, since she was alone so much of the time, with so few contacts with the world. So he had one delivered to her apartment. Another time, he sent her a check and told her to buy herself a fur coat, which she dutifully did, though it hung on her in the way of all her other baggy coats, thereby looking less elegant than he'd no doubt intended.

One of his more singular amusements was to pay for the meals of total strangers, particularly women no longer young and not terribly pretty; he would instruct the waiter to bring him their bill and tell them an admirer had taken care of it. Then he would pat my hand: "I couldn't have done that if I were here alone. Emilio would take me for a dirty old man."

Twenty minutes later, though, he might be pounding the table and roaring at me—for wearing textured stockings, for wasting my time and my father's money on the study of English literature, for going on a peace march: "What do you know about this war? You just enjoy getting together with the others and screaming like banshees. Next time, they should throw you in jail with the rest of the criminals and let you rot."

"It's called civil disobedience, Uncle Hans; it's not exactly like robbing old ladies in alleyways. Are you really telling me you can't see the difference?"

"Of course it is the same—they are criminals, criminals, and you are a criminal, too." The people at the nearby tables would stare at us, his friends the waiters would hover solicitously—I was sure they would never intervene if he slugged me, only if it were the other way around—while we glared at each other with pure hatred, a perfect genetic communion of bad temper.

But the worst explosion I ever provoked from him was about the Germans. The year I was seventeen, he had taken my sister and me to Europe for a Grand Tour, and we were spending a week in Paris. On our last night in town, a man who worked for my father had invited us out for dinner, and in the course of the evening he and his wife had told us about their experiences during the war. They had been hidden in a barn by Polish farmers, while their infant daughter was locked in a closet, so that her spine and legs never grew properly; she still needed crutches and a brace. It was the first time I had heard a story like that from someone who had actually lived it. Walking back to our hotel, brooding over what they'd told us, I said reproachfully to my uncle, "I don't see how you can not hate the Germans."

He grabbed me without warning, shaking me so ferociously that the wind was knocked out of me, and screamed that they hadn't known, they hadn't known, nobody had told them what was really going on; the Nazis were only the scum, the German people had hated them, too, but what could they do, they had the guns; it was my precious English who had invented concentration camps . . . my sister, always anxious to please him, chimed in on his side, but he only shushed her frantically and went on talking, shouting, offering up all the justifications for the Germans that the Germans themselves—though I did not know this at the time—were wont to give. The words poured out in a flood, as though they had been lying in wait for years, decades; as though, at three in the morning, when he could not sleep, these were the arguments he conjured up to ward off the horror. He seemed hardly to pause for breath, or to notice I was there.

And for once I was too frightened to shout back. I stood there paralyzed, waiting for sanity to return, until finally, abruptly, he released me and marched off in the direction of our hotel. But I had learned a certain measure of prudence. When we arrived, a few days later, at the Grand Hotel in Nuremberg, the city where my father and uncle had been born, I pretended not to notice the scars on the cheek of the obsequious desk clerk who greeted Hans by name; nor did I mention the creepy middle-aged man who had followed me when I went out alone, and how I had burst into tears and called him a Nazi.

My uncle took us to see the *Gymnasium* he and my father had attended, from which he had nearly been expelled for dangling his feet out a window; the narrow street where they had lived with their parents; their grandfather's incongruously lacy, French-looking villa, just inside the city's old wall. Here my great-grandfather had entertained Crown Prince Rupprecht of Bavaria, who had conferred on him certain honorary titles for his services to the court. We went to the Albrecht-Dürer-Haus and the Biergartens, where the professionally jolly waiters laughed with Hans about our failure to drink up, and we gagged over headcheese and something concocted from pigs' bladders. We accompanied him to his tailor, and to the shop from which he always bought his old-fashioned shirts with the detachable collars. We made excursions to the opera house in Munich and to Neuschwanstein and Herrenchiemsee, the castles of the mad King Ludwig.

But never did we go to Dachau, from which my mother's father had carried his dying brother in 1939, and from which my favorite cousin had rescued her husband in 1938 by bringing his medals from the 1914–18 war to the police chief and persuading him to intervene. We were pretending that German history was all Schiller and Kaiser Wilhelm and Frederick Barbarossa, that Nuremberg was simply a great medieval city, not the home of *Der Stürmer*, the site of those vast rallies in the thirties, a place that had given its name to the infamous laws restricting the rights of Jews and half-Jews, quarter-Jews, and Jews married to Gentiles in Hitler's Reich. The Tourist Authority of the Federated Republic, whose brochures so assiduously promoted the same impression, should have given us an award.

Yet the longer we stayed in Germany, embroidering our lie of omission, the gloomier my uncle became, sinking further and further into silence, until even I began to feel a little sorry for him. He would sit in a café, staring out over the square, and sigh heavily; he would gaze morosely down certain alleyways we passed, or at certain windows of old buildings, removing his glasses and rubbing the bridge of his nose like someone wiping away tears. What was he thinking of? Was he grieving for the victims of genocide or only the ordinary passing of a childhood world?

The rest of the family, too, had emigrated with their leather-bound volumes of Goethe and their prized recordings of Beethoven's string quartets. Presumably they did not throw out the Lebkuchen and Bratwurst that Hans sent them on his periodic trips back, but none of them indulged in this shameful nostalgia for Germany. Perhaps they disapproved of it as I did, finding it undignified or worse: to them, it was a point of honor not to keep pining for a country that had spurned them. For that was what my uncle was like—a spurned and stricken lover, unable to believe that his beloved had turned on him with such viciousness, trying to cast the murderous facts in a more palatable light.

It is possible to imagine him—the eldest son of the favored son, destined to inherit the Frenchified villa and the best Meissen and his father's decorations for bravery—feeling some particular streak of patriotism, a special allegiance to the country his father had fought for. And it is possible to discern, in his lifelong fascination with the heroic past—he had been a passionate amateur Egyptologist, serving as a consultant to the Kaiser Friedrich Museum in Berlin—some strain of romanticism that made him more susceptible to the Teutonic myths than any Jew should have been. Apart from that, it is difficult to see why he, of all the family, should have clung so desperately to the idea of Germany. They had all thought of themselves as Germans, after all, that being the only identity they'd been taught. None of them had been given religious training, celebrated Jewish holidays, attended a synagogue except for weddings and funerals—and even weddings, as in my uncle's case, were often civil affairs, since many of the family married Gentiles. They had prided themselves on their assimilation; Germanness had pervaded their lives; and suddenly permission was withdrawn, they were not allowed to be

German any longer. Yet, of all of them, Hans was the one who wound up sitting in a crowded café in Nuremberg in a state of such palpable loneliness that he seemed to be surrounded by vast and desolate space. He was the one trying, in the city of his birth, to buy the friendship of waiters with extravagant tips.

After that trip to Germany, I went off to college and my uncle resumed his travels, so that we saw each other very infrequently, and always with disastrous results. That was the period of my textured stockings and protest marches, so that our lunches could be counted on to end in an eruption. Once he actually ordered me out of a restaurant, because I had told him I loved Oscar Wilde.

He would sometimes phone my mother, always at eight in the morning, which he must have considered a perfectly reasonable hour. When she got those early-morning calls from him, she told me, and he began a sentence with "My niece," she knew he was talking about my sister; when he started with "Your daughter," it was always about me. Thus, she was informed at eight one morning about the peace march: "Did you know that your daughter went to Washington last weekend with a bunch of other hooligans?" (My mother did know, and was all in favor; she was as much against the war in Vietnam as I was.) Or "Your daughter has lost the check I gave her for her birthday, and I had to give her another one." Worst of all, "Your daughter has run away from Heidelberg, where I had sent her to learn German, and gone to work as a farmhand in England." (This was after my junior year abroad.) My mother would do her feeble best to defend me, though her attempt on that last occasion in particular was a further source of annoyance to Hans; when I had returned to America, he reported to me in a tone of outrage that after I had absconded from Germany, my mother had told him, "Evie loves the English language so much, I don't think she can ever really adapt to another one." This he regarded as the most nonsensical statement he'd ever heard.

And I was just as unsympathetic to him. When my father reported to me, during my final year in college, that Hans could no longer travel as he used to, because his wife was sick with "hardening of the arteries" and he would not leave her, I said meanly that it served my uncle right. After years of doing exactly as her husband wanted, of never daring to interfere with his plans, my submissive aunt was exacting a sort of revenge.

If my father had not gotten cancer, and I had not left my rich husband, I might hardly have had any further contact with my uncle. But the two events in combination brought me back to New York when I was twenty-four. I had been shocked to find that nobody I knew thought my righteous decision not to take any of my husband's millions away from him was a wise idea. Not only had my father threatened to hire an *amicus curiae* to intervene, but even various of my friends from college, whose lives of poverty in the East Village I had regarded as more virtuous than my own, told me I was being a fool and kept urging me to change my mind.

My uncle was the very last person I expected to appreciate the subtle point of honor involved. On the day he came to visit me in my dingy apartment on Tenth Street—inspecting the place, I knew, at my father's behest—I braced myself for the worst explosion yet. But all he did was look around mournfully, hand me an enormous parcel of tea and lingonberry jam and Bahlsen cookies, and ask whether my husband hadn't at least offered to give me something to tide me over. I said that he hadn't, which was true—he had only offered me various inducements (an English sports car, a full Freudian analysis) if I would stay. My uncle looked stern. "Then of course you can't ask him for anything. It's very bad to take money from a stingy person."

In retrospect, I am not sure he had hit on a maxim to live by, but at the time I felt as though I had received a benediction. For the first time ever, he was on my side. And during the year that followed—while my father was shunted from one hospital to another, radiated and burned and poisoned, his leg hacked away still further; while my uncle's wife, afflicted with what must have been Alzheimer's, withered away in a nursing home in Westchester, moaning for him constantly when he was absent but moaning just as much when he was there—my uncle and I arrived at a truce that would prove to be lasting. Occasionally there were still the old outbursts—when

I changed jobs, for example, and he, who had never shown much fondness for jobs, roared at me that I had no *Sitzfleisch*, no *Sitzfleisch* at all—but mostly we were awkwardly, fussily gentle with each other, full of lame solicitude. If one of us so much as sneezed, the other would cluck and fret and propose remedies like a mother hen—hardly the customary practice in our family.

When the weather permitted, we might go for long strolls in the park on Sunday afternoons, he in his high-topped, glossy black shoes, with the funny rounded toes and the little hooks instead of holes for the laces, which he ordered from a shoemaker in Zurich, I in battered sneakers of which he surely disapproved. Once he persuaded me to come with him to the opera, sometimes I met him for dinner after he'd been to visit his wife, but most of our time together was spent in the back of the car that took us out to Connecticut to see my father. My brother was away at college; my sister had already moved to Canada with her husband; my father's younger brother had died twelve years before. So apart from my stepmother, Hans and I were the family's chief attendants, constant visitors from New York to that suburban hospital where, until recently, my father had been launching the expansion program to link it to various teaching hospitals. Now his efforts were bearing fruit in his own case: the doctors connected to the place kept coming up with hopeful new suggestions, new leads to follow up about experimental treatments at Yale or Sloan Kettering or Dana-Farber.

They were always showing up in my father's hospital room with copies of the *New England Journal of Medicine*, write-ups about chemotherapy and radiation and hormone treatments, promises to phone the man in charge and ask him to see my father at once.

It was probably unfortunate that my husband had done a residency at a Harvard hospital, so that I could not regard such figures as infallible, especially since half the conversation among the interns and residents had consisted of horror stories about hospital screwups. I had heard about the anesthesiologist at Mass General who was late for a tennis date and so yanked the oxygen off someone before breathing function was restored, and the inept graduate of the medical school who had been thrown out of two internships elsewhere and then given a residency at Cambridge City, because Harvard looks after its own. Even worse, my favorite among my husband's old classmates used to fulminate against the oncologists, painting them as vultures always on the lookout for prey. They lied about their success rates, he said, in order to trick cancer patients into participating in their experiments; they recommended treatments based on their need to justify expensive radiation equipment they'd bought.

And there was my father, with his exaggerated diffidence in the face of other people's learning, his near-nineteenth-century faith in science and reason, Harvard degrees and human progress, thanking those men profusely for their efforts and signing on for one bout of torture after another. I could not tell him what my husband's friend had said—it would have been like saying he was doomed to die—but every time they tried one of those treatments and failed, every time they burned or poisoned him or cut him open to no avail, I remembered the story of the falsified success rates. My father had taken on a look of dazed suffering, a sort of terrible, mute patience that made me hate those doctors more and more.

Only to my uncle could I express such feelings, he having also no faith in doctors and science, or American know-how in general (the treatment he'd chosen for his varicose veins was to be leeched by an elderly doctor in Switzerland). Together we grieved for my father's innocence, his humility, as though he were our trusting virgin daughter being seduced before our eyes. We looked on helplessly, unable to protect him, as these men showed up to offer their blandishments, and then vented our bitterness on the ride back.

"What do you think they would have done if he'd been the local mailman? Do you think they would have given him this new treatment?"

"No."

"So: they let the mailman die in peace, and your father is put on the rack. But this Dr. Castilaw seems pleased with the new treatment. What did you think of him?"

"I thought he was a self-important jerk like all the others. A real Harvard asshole."

"You shouldn't use that language; your husband won't like it."

"But I don't have a husband, Uncle Hans."

"When you have one, he won't like it." He sighed. "You'll marry a marine biologist in Corpus Christi, Texas, and I'll never see you anymore."

"I'll come visit you."

"Not very often. What will I do when I'm old and sick and need to be put out of my misery? Who's going to shoot me if you're not around? Your sister will never do it."

Finally, when the doctors had stopped suggesting new treatments, when they started to withdraw from the picture, and my father requested they do nothing further to keep him alive, he kept slipping in and out of high fevers. We could never know, when we went to see him, if he would be awake or asleep, or if he would recognize us when his eyes opened. And in the final week of his life, he, too, began returning to Germany, inquiring about trains to Stuttgart, imagining I was visiting him from Heidelberg, where their younger brother had gone to university. Once, it being winter, I arrived at the hospital in high leather boots, and pointing at them, he said faintly, "*So wie die SS.*"

Unlike my uncle, my father had been so much part of American life, so busy with civic projects, so concerned with what lay ahead rather than behind, that I had hardly ever thought of him as an immigrant. Now his German brother was reclaiming him, bearing him back into their past. More and more, they spoke together in German, my uncle bending over the bed, my father, half-conscious, whispering things I could not understand. Watching them, I felt an enormous loneliness, although whose it was, I could not be sure—whether my own, at seeing my father die in a foreign language; or my father's, at the nearness of death; or some distillation of how the two of them must have felt once, the old loneliness of being cast out from everything they had known.

On almost our last ride back from the hospital, at two in the morning, Hans said to me, "Do you know what I am? The Generation of the Desert. Do you know about them?" I didn't. "They are the ones who wandered in the desert for forty years but could not get to the Promised Land, the ones who kept saying to Moses, 'Why did you ever bring us out of Egypt? Things were so much better in Egypt.' Your father got to America, he arrived in the Promised Land, but I never did."

There was no answer I could make; I reached out my hand, and he took it, and then we both stared out the car windows, watching the wind make shadows of the trees on the Merritt Parkway.

Not long after my father's death, Hans's wife died, too, and a year later he announced that he was marrying again. His future bride was another German Jewish refugee, a childless widow who seemed surprisingly

100

determined to get her own way. So Hans was finally persuaded to give up the apartment where he had lived since
arriving in America, and to move into her larger one; not
only that, it seemed she did not want him to bring his furniture with him—admittedly, having been bought when he
first immigrated, it was mostly of very cheap wood, flimsy
pine, and after years of use it had sagged or split in ways
that any proud housewife might have objected to. But she
also had her own china, and so he asked me if I would like
the blue-and-white Meissen, in the famous apple-and-on-
ion design, that had once belonged to my grandmother;
she had sent it to him in what was then Czechoslovakia,
where he'd emigrated in 1936, thinking it a safe haven
from the Nazis. It was a complete set, with large and small
serving platters, a huge soup tureen, a dozen soup bowls
and dinner plates and dessert plates, two coffeepots, a
teapot, many milk or cream jugs of various sizes, and half
a dozen covered receptacles for vegetables; some of the
smaller plates were edged with delicate fretwork. It has
remained one of the few possessions I treasure and look
after as he might have wanted; I have wrapped every piece
separately in newspaper for each of my many moves, and
always made sure that it arrived safely.

He would have it professionally packed and sent to
me, Hans said, but he wanted me to come to his apartment and see if there was anything else I wanted, such as
the pots and pans his first wife had used to cook him the
German delicacies he preferred. (I was especially taken

with a Pyrex double boiler.) And he explained to me, as he showed me the Meissen, which was merely the "kitchen china" and which the really fine porcelain; the kitchen Meissen was slightly thicker, in a brighter blue, with "Villeroy & Boch, Dresden" inscribed on the underside, whereas on the underside of each item of porcelain, there was a pair of crossed swords.

He seemed mellower that day, more un-Hans-like, than I had ever seen him, a little lost, even—not unhappy exactly, but less sure of himself. Maybe it was the prospect of leaving the place that had been home for so long, a home he had shared for forty years with his wife; maybe it was some inkling he had that with his new wife he was not going to have everything his way, that it would be her wishes that would prevail. I think he already sensed that the marriage was not going to be an unqualified success.

Once we had gone through the kitchen things, and I had told him which of them I'd like to have, we sat in his living room for the last time; he was looking a little bereft, and fell silent. "When you marry at my age," he said, "it's for companionship." I nodded. And then he asked me, which he never had before, whether I had a boyfriend.

Yes, I told him, I did.

"What does he do?" he wanted to know, and I hesitated.

"You're not going to like this, Uncle Hans."

"What? Is he a criminal? A Communist?"

"No," I said. "He's a poet."

102

"You mean he writes poems?"

"Yes."

"How horrible."

I met his second wife only once, when her sister gave them a wedding lunch at her house in Flushing on the day of their marriage. I felt weirdly humble at the prospect of meeting not the new wife but her sister, who had been in Auschwitz and been sterilized in one of Dr. Mengele's experiments. So it was baffling to me, once we had all sat down, to hear her chatting away about food and shopping and the show she and her husband had just seen on Broadway—to realize that the horrors in her past, which I could not get out of my mind, were far from her own thoughts as she emerged from the kitchen with the iced layer cake she had made for dessert. I kept watching her for signs that she was merely putting on a brave front, but I could detect nothing of that, no tragic aura clinging to her.

Shortly after Hans's marriage I left for England, planning to live there on a modest allowance my mother had given me that was equal to the interest my sister and brother-in-law would have paid her on the money she'd given them for the house in Canada. The idea was that I would try seriously, for the first time ever, to write, though only my mother knew of that plan. I can't remember what I told Hans I intended to do, but when I had been in London for just a few months, my sister wrote to me and told me that he was in the hospital with stomach cancer, and wasn't expected to live. So I bought a cheap plane ticket and returned to New York to say good-bye.

When I entered his hospital room, he was in the middle of lunch, which was not a tray of mush and milk, such as might have been served to patients with stomach cancer, but a scallop of veal and a *crème brûlée* that he'd had delivered from one of his favorite restaurants. "Since I am going to die anyway," he told me cheerfully, "I may as well enjoy a few decent meals before I depart." The nurses, of course, were grumbling about it; they told me it was strictly against hospital rules, an outrageous breach of protocol, but apparently the doctor had told them to let him have his way—after all, the meals they had wanted to serve him would no more cure his cancer than the gourmet delights he insisted on. Nor did he seem to suffer any worse pains after eating his extravagant meals than when they had foisted the hospital food on him.

Having been told that the chances of success were not great, he had refused the treatments the doctors had suggested. "I saw too much of that with your father," he said. And then he told me that the reason he hadn't returned to Nuremberg since he'd taken my sister and me to see it was that he'd realized then that, however scrupulously it was rebuilt after the heavy Allied bombing, it could never again be the city he had known. "It was like a Disneyland version of the Nuremberg I remember. Nobody can ever bring it back."

I did not say, although I thought it, that it was his dream of Germany that could not be brought back; I did not say that it had all been a lie, the seductive offer the Germans had made to the Jews before the Nazis came to power—telling them, in effect, "It's a terrible thing to be Jewish, but we won't make you be; we'll let you be German instead: enlightened, cultured, dignified, prosperous, too. We'll give you this world instead of the other one." And then it was stripped away from them, leaving them with nothing at all.

I would like to believe that if I had been living then, I would have known better, I would have seen that the striving for assimilation was rooted in shame, that all the snobbery about the *Ostjuden* amounted to a hatred of what we were. But the truth is I, too, might have tried to out-German the Germans; I might have been guilty of every sin of which their co-religionists accused the *yekkes*: arrogance, snobbery, betrayal of their heritage, selling their birthright for a mess of second-rate mythologies and sentimental poems. There's no way of knowing who I would have been, what I would have believed, in that place and time.

But when I remember my uncle in Nuremberg, I seem to recognize the expression on his face, incomprehensible to me when I was seventeen. It was bewilderment at the vagaries of history, at what had been done to him, which was so much less than what was done to so many others, and yet enough to leave him marooned for life.

CHAPTER FOUR: *The Pioneers*

The most remarkable member of my family was undoubtedly my father's younger brother, my Uncle George–Georg in Germany, Giora in Israel, where there are hospitals and schools and streets bearing his name. In 1960, when I was nine years old, he was in New York to address the American Jewish Committee about funding for new irrigation projects, and he came to the apartment for dinner. He had a large, expansive presence, with a booming laugh like Hans's, but warmer, less harsh; it was impossible to imagine him losing his temper the way Hans did. He seemed so genuinely interested in me, something I hadn't expected, even wanting to hear about the books I was reading (the Brontë sisters').

What I didn't know then was that for all his air of relaxed sociability, my uncle had spent much of his early life committing dangerous and even illegal acts: raising money for arms for the Haganah, the banned Jewish self-defense group–which ultimately became the Israeli army–in what was then Palestine, and smuggling the money he'd raised in Europe into the country under the noses of the British authorities; at various times, he may have smuggled guns and ammunition, too. And that was just the beginning: later he became a people-smuggler, managing to get thousands of European Jews into Palestine both before and after the war, despite the British Mandate's prohibition on any further Jewish settlement.

When I read a biography of him years later—I never saw him again; he died of a heart attack at the age of fifty—I realized that he must have been the black sheep of the family back then, a rebel like me, though unlike me one with a cause. Not only had he been a committed socialist and an early Zionist, he had even refused to celebrate Christmas with the family, or to decorate the tree with them, something they had done throughout his youth. And my grandparents had been horrified when he'd become engaged to a woman he'd met in a Zionist group. Apparently they'd asked him, "Are you really going to marry that *shtetl* Jew?" It was a particularly unfair slur on his proposed wife, since her family had lived in Germany almost as long as theirs; the only difference was that they actually practiced their religion, which to my proudly assimilated grandparents was a source of embarrassment.

And although he had a law degree, graduating from the University of Berlin the same year the Nazis came to power, my uncle never practiced law as they'd expected. Instead, even as a student, he'd devoted himself to doing social work among the poor, which he continued doing when he'd completed his studies. Over the next few years, he switched his focus to retraining thousands of young German Jews to become useful workers—farmers, toolmakers, carpenters—in Palestine, another clandestine activity, since it could never be publicly acknowledged that such was the purpose of the workshops and farm camps he established outside Berlin and Munich. In 1936, he was appointed the head of this "Pioneer" movement for all of Germany. I doubt that that was a source of pride to my grandparents either, since like many German Jews, they were firm believers that one day their fellow Germans would come to their senses, get rid of Hitler, and stop persecuting all their loyal Jewish citizens.

Despite their opposition, my uncle married his "little *shtetl* Jew," and in 1987, twenty-five years after his death, I met her for the first time when she came to America to give fundraising speeches to Jewish organizations in New York; afterward, making the rounds of her American relatives, she visited my husband and me in our house in northern Vermont.

It was October, the trees were at their gorgeous peak, all red and gold and purple, but when we took her on a drive around the back roads, she didn't even comment on them. It was only as we circled the vastness of Lake Willoughby that she asked us to stop the car for a minute, looking awestruck. "So much water," she said wistfully. It was the most emotion she showed during the whole of the visit, and brought home to me more forcefully than any film I'd seen or book I'd read that Israel was a desert country.

Over dinner in our house, she and my husband had a lengthy discussion of Middle Eastern politics, about which he knew much more than I did, being an avid reader of newspapers, which I was not. I remember that she was very angry about the settlements being established on the West Bank, and the treatment of the Palestinians in general; she despised the right-wing government of the day; she had protested outside the Knesset, she had signed petitions.

For all their fierce Zionism, she and Giora had always been in favor of a two-state solution, she said at the dinner table. "Only the Arabs rejected it. But still, we believed in our vision of what Israel could be. Giora was among those in the Mapai [the socialist democratic party] who argued for equal rights for the Arabs who remained in Israel. It brought him into conflict with Ben-Gurion, but he would not back down. 'Israel must not treat the Palestinians the way the Nazis treated the Jews'—that was what he said. And I always supported him. We believed in Israel as a socialist state, that was not just a dream for us, but now it is getting very far from that."

At the end of that dinner, when my grandmother's clock chimed ten, she stood up from the table, looked at her watch as though to ensure it was accurate, and said, "So. We go for a walk tomorrow morning, yes? At eight o'clock sharp." After she'd marched off to bed, my WASP husband said mournfully, "You think when you marry a Jew, you're going to be part of this warm, loving family

109

that hugs you and tells you great stories and gives you delicious things to eat. I got a bunch of Krauts."

We did not, after all, go for a walk at precisely eight o'clock the next morning, but a little later, when we'd finished breakfast, I took her tromping through the hilly fields around our house—empty now of our neighbor's cows, the grazing season being over—and managed to get her talking not just about Giora, as she always called him, but her own life. Like him, she had gone to university to study law; like him, she'd been involved in preparing German Jews for emigration to Palestine, "but it was the young women I was working with; with the help of some of them, I established a training farm near Berlin." Also like him, she had smuggled both guns and money from Germany into the Palestine of the British Mandate: "They thought women made much better smugglers, because nobody would suspect them. So we used to get dressed in very proper clothes, we even wore high-heeled shoes and hats with feathers, imagine, and almost always we got through safely. Then we'd hand over the shoes and the hats to the girls who were bringing the bullets to the Haganah."

That was during the late '30s, during which time, she explained, Giora was raising money to purchase a number of old, rickety ships to take Jewish emigrants from Rotterdam and Antwerp to Palestine. From long lists of applicants who had completed their "pioneer" training, he was responsible for choosing those he felt would be the best workers, and best able to stand the harsh conditions in a desert country.

Of course, the emigration program he initiated was in direct contravention of the British ban on further Jewish settlement (in 1939, the British had issued a White Paper limiting Jewish immigration to 15,000 a year, and the emigrants had to disembark into fishing boats in Haifa to elude the British blockade). It was not the British, though, who arrested him at that point but, several times in 1937, the Gestapo, who had evidence showing that he was connected to the Haganah. Walking beside me, our shoulders sometimes brushing up against one another due to the uneven terrain, Senta said drily, "Their methods of interrogation were not so advanced then, and Giora was able to withstand them. One of them, in a later meeting with another Zionist, even remarked on how his courage and clear thinking had commanded their respect." They did, however, retain his passport, so that he'd be available for further questioning. But in 1938, the district commissioner, without checking with Berlin, issued him a new passport, impressed by his being a doctor of law.

"Did he ever go back to Germany after that?" I asked.

She shook her head. "He couldn't risk returning there, but to other parts of Europe, yes. He made many such journeys, back and forth from Palestine; we all knew the time was getting short: more documents were needed, more money, more ships. He joined a mission that met with representatives of the Western European countries, trying to persuade them to open their borders to young German Jews, if only until they could get to Palestine. But in the spring of 1939 what I had been dreading happened—he was arrested again, in Paris this time, by the French police. They searched his case and found a hundred passports, all forged of course, and put him in prison. But some Jewish friends in Paris with connections to the government managed to get him released, and he returned to Palestine."

"How could they possibly have managed that?" I asked, incredulous. "I mean, he had one hundred fake passports in his possession. That's got to be a major crime."

She shrugged. "I don't know how they did it; they must have bribed someone. But we realized then that it was too dangerous for him to keep returning to Europe."

She bent down to scrape some wet straw off one of the hiking boots that I'd lent her. "And then I left Germany for good and joined him in Palestine; we had decided to make our permanent home there. But before settling down, we decided to visit a training farm in Poland. We believed that some familiarity with Polish He-Halutz [a Jewish youth movement that trained young people for agricultural work in Palestine] would make it easier to understand Palestine and especially the kibbutz. During the Holocaust, Giora often told me how grateful he was to have had some contact, however brief, with this Jewry before its destruction." Shortly after that trip to Poland, war broke out. "All his life," Senta said, "he was haunted by the thought of those he hadn't chosen to go on those ships. He knew that his decisions about who would or wouldn't be suited to life on a kibbutz had meant death for those left behind."

I thought Senta might like to see the alpacas a friend of mine was raising, and I led her through a short stretch of woods filled with Douglas fir toward a small farm with a painted outbuilding much smaller than a barn. Pointing to it, Senta said, "When Giora and I first settled in Palestine, our home was much smaller than that; it was actually a chicken hut we shared with six other people." I must have made some noise expressing dismay, at which she turned to me and told me impatiently that they hadn't complained; they were just happy to have a place to live. "Later, when we moved into a tent, and only had to share with one other immigrant, we felt we were living in luxury. But we weren't allowed to join the left-wing kibbutz when we made an application; they said German Jews were too spoiled to fit into kibbutz life. If only they had seen how we'd been living before!" (Another version of the story, told to me by an Israeli, was that the German Jews could not get along with their Eastern brethren because their habits were too different: the Eastern Jews were not as efficient and disciplined as the Germans.)

As Senta boldly approached a pair of alpacas and began stroking their noses, it occurred to me to ask, "How did you support yourselves?"

"We commuted from where we were living–in the tent–to work on several other kibbutzes, but Giora was so clumsy–such a klutz–that he not only broke some tools, he managed to break his ankle, too."

That I could easily believe, since our whole family was hopeless when it came to any sort of practical task. A neighbor of ours in Connecticut had once said, fondly, that my father couldn't hit a nail if it had the instructions on the head in Latin. But Senta didn't seem particularly amused when I told her that. Unlike her husband, whom many people described as having a lively sense of humor–I would see proof of it in some of the letters quoted in his biography–that was not one of her more marked characteristics.

Instead, as we continued our walk, she went on to tell me proudly that she had been a much more useful worker. "For two years during the war, while Giora was in Cairo [having volunteered for the British Army, he was made an intelligence officer, an interrogator of German prisoners of war], I worked as a milkmaid for an old couple. This, I enjoyed very much indeed, to work with animals.

"Ever since, I have had a special affinity for cows. I am very sorry not to have seen these American cows while I am here." I wondered if it could possibly have been the cows' docility she felt an affinity with, since she seemed anything but docile herself.

Throughout that visit, I could never decide if I liked her or not; I only knew she made me feel humble, a

114

smaller person than she was. Living in a chicken hut with six other people, uncomplainingly no less: that would have been beyond me. And I had never devoted my life to a cause as she had, unless you counted the egotistical pursuit of trying to write something decent. (She never asked me anything about my writing, or commented on the paintings of my husband that hung on the walls of our house, much less complimented me on the elaborate meal I had prepared for dinner, complete with a lemon meringue pie for dessert. Clearly, such things were of no interest to her; the only thing that mattered was the fate of Israel.)

Following long negotiations, she told me, her employers agreed to sell their cows to a kibbutz that Senta was trying to establish on land in Ramot Menashe in northern Israel. But the Arab sharecroppers who used that land for grazing their animals protested; only when the money was found to compensate both them and the owners of the land, after the war, could the planned kibbutz for German Jews be established at last. There Senta and Giora settled, though he could only intermittently be in residence with her, having been asked on his discharge from the army to form an "absorption department" of the Jewish Agency.

There is a quote in Giora's biography from his address to the first Zionist Congress to be held in Jerusalem: "We are continuing to take in the waves of mass immigration and to conduct a desperate campaign against a shortage of raw materials and means of production, a shortage of funds, and a shortage of trained personnel." (He also said, "Let us preserve the best values each community brings us. Each group has a positive tradition in some sphere or other." And yet many years later, in 2018, a street in Netanya that bore his name was renamed for Bracha Tzfira, an Israeli singer of North African origin, because a documentary film of 2017 revealed that Giora had once characterized the North African Jews as "an immigration with poor moral weight, a lesser social level . . . they may bring the country down to the depths of a Levantine society." So it seems that, democratic socialist that he was, even he was not entirely immune to the prejudices of the German Jews about Jews from the East and from North Africa.)

"When he first started at the adoption agency," Senta told me, "he still had to circumvent the immigration restrictions the British tried to enforce. But that wasn't the main problem he faced. He was working sixteen, eighteen, twenty hours a day to provide the new arrivals with doctors, nurses, teachers, blankets, milk . . . and canvas tents to live in."

"It doesn't sound as though you ever got to spend much time together," I said to Senta. "That must have been hard."

But she did not want my sympathy. "We had other priorities. Someone had to take charge of the reception and settlement of the remnants of European Jewry who wanted to come to Palestine. And I knew that Giora was the best person to do that. So I helped him all I could. We were particularly concerned with the leaky roofs of so many of those tents, and we kept trying to find solutions to the problem. He was desperate to find the money to build real houses for them, so he kept going back and forth to America, to drum up financial help from Jewish organizations there."

His biography also told of his leading role in the negotiations with the Germans after the war, and how reluctant he'd been to take it on. It must have been a horribly distasteful task, sitting in a conference room in Holland opposite representatives of the German Federal Republic, haggling for money. Nor could he go in the confidence that the whole country was behind him. Many Israelis felt a similar repugnance: it was obscene, they said, to accept money, German gold, as "reparations" for those six million deaths. And it would only reinforce the idea in the minds of anti-Semites that the Jews cared about nothing but money. There was a big uproar about it in the Knesset, and protests erupted throughout the country.

But the fact was, Israel's finances were in terrible shape; there was not nearly enough in the treasury to feed and house and train all those immigrants pouring into the country to escape the nightmare that Europe had become for them. Ben-Gurion pleaded with Giora to change his mind—he'd had legal training in Germany, after all; they needed someone with an understanding of German law—and finally he agreed. But according to one of his biographers, it was with "a very heavy heart."

Throughout the months that the negotiations went on, in a castle fifteen miles outside The Hague that had been converted into a hotel, he wrote to Senta whenever he had a free hour, which was not often. Here, as quoted in his biography, is his description of the first day the delegates met:

"The encounter was a dramatic one. Everyone got up when we came in. Nobody shook hands with anybody but just bowed mutely when introduced. After the statements had been read . . . the Germans left the room with deep bows. Police in front of the castle, plainclothes men outside the conference room, police in the hotel lobby and all over the grounds. It is all unreal. The Germans are unreal too, for they represent the best aspects of the Weimar Republic and not the Germany of the past twenty years. And I don't know how much influence they have in Bonn."

And in the same letter: "Keep smiling. Hanni sent some coffee for you, but not much, because no more is allowed."

The Germans had many other creditors, the British and the Americans among them; to get anything close to even half the amount (a billion dollars) the Israelis had initially requested, Giora had to persuade those other creditors to take less, or to wait longer for their money, or to lend Israel money themselves. He kept having to travel

back and forth to London and America, and when he was
in The Hague, there were nightly phone calls at three in
the morning Dutch time, that being the only hour his US
liaison was free to talk to him. The Germans in Bonn,
Giora told Senta–"that filthy crew"–kept trying to "play
us off against the Americans. . . . we are not sure that we
can win."

During a trip to London, where the matter was pre-
sented to the British Parliament, and he visited the House
of Lords, he wrote to her, "I am not pessimistic, but one
ought to be able to buy nerves somewhere so as not to
lose this war. A few more rows and we shall squeeze
something out of them, provided that nothing unforeseen
happens."

In another letter: "Tomorrow we are going to light a
fire under the Germans to speed things up a bit. They
check back on every piddling thing, and this holds things
up. . . . It is high time for me to eat *tsenna* [literally, 'scar-
city' or 'austerity': the skimpy rations provided to Israeli
citizens at that time] again; I am beginning to turn into a
rootless Diaspora Jew." And finally, "after a number of
lucky breaks finally worked to our advantage, Bertha"–as
he called Bonn–"agreed to pay eight hundred million
dollars over a period of eight to twelve years, partly in
cash and partly in the form of credit for German goods."

Even all those years later, when I met her, Senta held
a grudge against Ben-Gurion, who had pressured Giora
not only to take charge of negotiating with the Germans,

but also, in 1956, to take on the role of the Mapai's general secretary, which meant overhauling its unwieldy party machine. In Senta's eyes, it was the stress of that job–"he hated every minute of it; he had always hated party politics"–that had brought on Giora's massive heart attack in 1959, at the age of forty-six. (I can't help thinking that his overeating, lack of exercise, and chain-smoking might have played a part, too: in practically every photograph I've seen of him, there was a cigarette in his mouth or his hand.)

Later that year, though, he was elected to the Knesset, and Ben-Gurion made him Minister of Labor. "That was a job," Senta said with satisfaction, "that he could finally throw himself into wholeheartedly." She went on to say that he pushed through legislation providing for social insurance and drafted a law addressing the needs of hand-icapped employees. Having previously argued for equal rights for Arabs as well as Jews, he attempted to include them in his provisions.

"But in 1961, he had another heart attack, and Hans insisted that he must have a rest. He invited us, or really commanded us–he was still the older brother, after all–to join him in a villa in Lucerne that he had rented for Giora's sake. All the signs were good, even the doctors thought Giora was recovering well, and encouraged his belief that he would soon be able to return to Israel and get down to work again. He was counting the days, he had so many plans for what he wanted to do." But, as I knew, he never did go back: after they had been in Switzerland for not quite two weeks, Giora had another heart attack and died.

As we rounded a corner of a field and started back in the direction of my house, I asked Senta how she'd coped after Giora's death. "I went back to the kibbutz, of course," she said, though her time there was interrupted by two terms in the Knesset in the 1970s—"I didn't care at all for political life, they asked me to run for a third term, but I refused"—and her work as head of the Israeli Federation of Trade Unions. In 1978, she'd returned to the kibbutz for good, working first in the cowshed—"I enjoyed that very much"—and then on the production line in the plastics factory that she'd helped to establish. That was where she was employed when she visited us in Vermont, and the job she'd continue in until her retirement at the age of eighty-eight. She died, aged ninety-four, in 2007, without my ever seeing her again.

After her visit, we kept in touch intermittently, though I struggled to find things to write about in my letters: art and literature or even news of my sister's and brother's children would clearly not have been subjects of much interest. So I would ask my husband for bulletins on what was happening in Israel and hope to sound intelligent about it, knowing that her country's well-being, the struggle to preserve something of how she'd once envisioned it, would always be Senta's one true passion. Later in my life, the memory of her single-mindedness, her absolute commitment, could even lead me to regard what was called "terrorism" in a slightly different light.

Even the undoubted love between her and Giora had been grounded in their shared devotion to the cause; when they were alone, I suspect they talked more about the problems confronting Israel than their personal feelings, although his letters to her from The Hague are full of little endearments and teases. ("My dear, you are in the best of company: we are colossal bankrupts. . . . You are a dear as well as a good letter writer. Write more and give me some political gossip.") I got no sense that she regretted the children she didn't have, the house she had never owned, or the comfort and ease she had never experienced.

If she considered anything at all memorable about her time with us, it would probably have been her discussions with my husband about Israeli politics and the sight of Lake Willoughby. Nor did she show any desire to see more of America. To her, its importance was wholly as a source of financial and political support for her country. Though she was not so blunt as to say it outright, she probably regarded Americans, Jewish or not, as self-indulgent, money-obsessed consumers, people without a real vision of anything beyond their comfortable lives.

But though I was clearly in that category, and therefore of no great interest to her apart from being Giora's niece, she was my only chance to find out about my grandparents, who had emigrated to Palestine in 1939. And knowing that the opportunity might not come again, at the end of our walk that day I pressed her for personal details about them, things she would undoubtedly never have thought to tell me without my urging. She answered my questions in the same matter-of-fact tone in which she had been discussing irrigation systems the night before, but at least she was willing to give me the facts. Despite my grandparents' initial disdain for her, on the somewhat peculiar grounds that she actually practiced their religion, they had soon come to accept her, she told me, and once they moved to Palestine, they developed a very warm relationship.

By this time we had made our circuit of the fields and had climbed the ridge behind our house, from where there was a spectacular view of the White Mountains of New Hampshire, sixty miles away. "Why," I asked her, puffing slightly, "did my grandparents choose to go there, rather than to New York, where they had two sons, and life was so much less harsh? My father had found sponsors for so many people, including my mother's parents, in his work with the refugee committees. Surely he could have found sponsors for them too."

"They preferred to come to us," she said briskly, "because they did not like your mother, and they did not like Mirl [Hans's wife]."

I didn't ask her why they'd disliked my mother; I didn't really want to hear the answer. But I did protest about Mirl: "What could they possibly have objected to about her? She was so meek and docile, such a perfect wife, she always did exactly what Hans wanted."

"Because," Senta said in her ringing voice, "she vas zo unpunctual." (Could that be the true reason the German Jews had to form their own kibbutz? Were the Eastern Jews too unpunctual?)

My grandfather, she told me, had gathered a group of young immigrants around him when he and my grand-mother arrived in Palestine in 1939. "He gave them reg-ular English lessons, and counseled them, too, as best as he could; he became a father figure for many of them. And he worked hard at learning Hebrew; he was so proud when finally he could read a Hebrew newspaper. He would tease Giora that his Hebrew was much better than Giora's, and it was true. Then war broke out, and he vol-unteered for the British Army; when they rejected him, he was very much upset." (He was seventy years old, his arm still crippled from the wound he had suffered while serv-ing in the German Army in the First World War.) "But still he wanted to be useful, so he insisted on doing active service in the Civil Guard." Nobody else had ever told me so much about him, and sparse though the facts were, I was greedy for every detail; she was giving me at least some inkling of what my grandfather had been like.

And what about my grandmother? I asked. At which point Senta told me something she had kept from my fa-ther and Hans, both of whom were dead by the time of her visit to us: Their mother had not died a natural death, as

Senta had pretended to them. Six months after my grand-father died of a heart attack, in 1943, she killed herself, slitting her wrists in the bath the day before her six-ty-eighth birthday. According to what Senta told me, she simply got into the communal bathtub when everyone else was out, armed with a razor. (Maybe she was even care-ful, given the shortage of water, not to run too deep a bath.)

Life in Tel Aviv in those years must have felt very grim to an upper-middle-class Jew from Nuremberg like my grandmother, who came from a more cultured and even more assimilated family than her husband's, who had nev-er been a convert to Zionism even in the worst years of the Nazi terror. Instead, she must have hoped and believed for as long as she possibly could that sanity would return to her country, that the madman Hitler would be ousted, and she could be a good German citizen again. It was a hope and belief that many people, not all of them Jews, clung to for at least the first five years of his reign. I asked Senta if, like my grandfather, my grandmother had tried to learn Hebrew: "No, never, she learned only the few phrases she needed to deal with the people in the gro-cery."

Everything about the country surely would have come as a shock to her. In the area of Tel Aviv where she lived, there were hardly any paved roads, there were camels walking in the streets. The heat was stifling, there were flies everywhere, clouds of dust flew up, she probably had to be very careful with the water she drew from the well, lest she be accused of taking more than her share. She, who years before had been the mistress of an *haut bourgeois* household, with a cook and several maids, was sharing a grungy kitchen with five other women, and the skimpy food they were cooking on the tiny stove was foreign to her: no more schnitzel, plum dumplings, Apfelstrudel, for which she had neither the money nor any chance of getting the ingredients. She couldn't even afford a radio, though my father, still a mere clerk in the import-export department of the pencil company, had taken on an extra job at night not only to pay off the debts my mother had incurred with her extravagance but to send as much money as possible to his relatives in Palestine. Maybe she realized that she had made a terrible mistake, that she and my grandfather should have gone to New York after all.

And however shameful it seems, I don't believe that her German Jewish snobbery had completely died just because the Nazis had lumped all Jews together into the category of *Untermenschen*. To be surrounded by Eastern European Jews, the *shtetl* Jews she and her kind had always viewed with distaste, must have made her feel even more alienated. No doubt they conversed among themselves in Yiddish, a language she would have regarded as a hideous bastardization of the *Hochdeutsch* spoken in her family.

Yet it can't have been just the company in which my grandmother found herself that drove her to suicide. At that point, it still looked as though the Germans might win the war. Rumors of what was happening in the concentration camps had begun to filter back. Since 1939, there had been no news of the close friends she'd parted from back in Germany. She had, however, received information that her only brother, a noted art historian, had killed himself on the Swiss border when he was refused entry because of the J stamped on his passport (the Swiss had had enough of Jewish refugees clamoring to be let in). Her husband had died a few months before. Maybe she felt that, like her brother, she had no future; in every meaningful sense her life was over, there was no point to being alive anymore. She may have thought she was nothing but a burden to her kindly youngest son, who however many hours he was working had always tried to make time for her, as did his equally overworked wife now that he was in Cairo with the British Army. If that was how it seemed to her, maybe she felt the kindest thing she could do for them was to relieve them of their obligation to fit her into their already crammed schedules.

"I was the one who found her body," Senta said, without even a catch in her voice, but she turned her head as she spoke, and stood looking at the blaze of color on the mountains in the distance. I didn't think to ask her if she had also lied about his mother's death to Giora; I wish I had.

But I did ask if my grandmother had left a note— hoping for some explanation, or maybe some final expression of love—and Senta said impatiently, "No, nothing. What would have been the point?" So I will never know what her reasons were; I will never know what went through her mind that day—if her last thoughts were of her sons, not just Giora but the other two, six thousand miles away, whose wives she found so objectionable.

Apart from the photograph of her on my father's dresser, I had had no image of her, no idea of what she was like, except what Hans had told me about her having to discipline her sons, my grandfather being reluctant ever to restrain or punish them. Since her face in the photograph had looked so severe and forbidding, I had found it easy to believe that. Yet Senta told me that my grandmother had, as she put it, "exceptionally good intuition about people"; it was from her, she said, that Giora had inherited his warmth, his sensitivity, and they had been extremely close. It was not just "the responsible attitude," then—the title given to his biography—that had made him find time for her despite his punishing work schedule. Which meant the stern-looking photograph of her in the house in Connecticut could not have been a true portrait, or at any rate a full one.

Years later, I saw another photograph of her, one my brother copied and sent to me. She is wearing a dark dress with an old-fashioned, high-necked lace collar that fans out over her shoulders; she doesn't look at all stern, only clear-eyed, thoughtful, surprisingly pretty (it was taken when she was still in her twenties, before the First World War). She could be an early suffragette, or equally someone I might have met at college. I can't see my own features in her face, but somehow she is familiar to me, a person I could have been friends with, had long discussions with into the night. She looks as though she'd have interesting things to say. She also looks as though she's full of hope for the future.

At first, I just tacked the photograph to the wall of my study with Blu-Tack. But one day I had an urge to do better by my grandmother, to honor her as she deserved. For weeks, it became almost an obsession to find just the right frame for that picture, and finally, after many trawls through antique shops, I found it: a plush velvet one, in olive green, with delicate silver curlicues at its corners. Her face now watches over me as I sit at my desk, and I see it each time I look up from my computer.

CHAPTER FIVE: *The Poetry Lover*

In the prettily carved desk in the room where she'd lived for almost thirty years, opposite the couch that became her bed at night, she kept a copy of an American men's magazine from the war years—decidedly not her usual sort of reading matter. But it contained an article about her husband, my father's cousin Fritz, who had volunteered for service in the German Army during the First World War, shortly after he and she were married; they had only a few months together before he was sent to France and made an officer, winning two Iron Crosses for his bravery in battle. (His only brother, also an officer, had already been killed in the fighting in France early in the war.) The article was about Fritz's confrontation with Julius Streicher, editor of the notorious anti-Semitic Nazi paper *Der Stürmer*. In 1923, when Fritz's father (my great-uncle), had just died, Streicher had published an article headlined something like "Jew Pig Dies" and claimed that the corpses of Gentile virgins and children had been found in "the Jew's" basement, their blood having been used for the Passover seder.

On the day the article appeared in *Der Stürmer*, Fritz went to its offices with a riding crop, pushed past the receptionist, and marched into Streicher's room. "Did you know Dr. Josephthal?" he demanded, and when Streicher said no, Fritz told him, "Then meet his son," lashing him across his face with the whip. Strangely, as the article pointed out, when the Nazis came to power ten years later, Streicher never sought revenge.

In fact, Fritz was one of the very few prominent Jews in Nuremberg who was not arrested and taken to Dachau on Kristallnacht, although he had become even more prominent since the Nazis took over: he and his law partner, a cousin of his, had been presenting legal arguments in court against the Aryanization of Jewish businesses and the arrest of fellow Jews. They never won any of those cases, but they did bring wider public attention to some of the Nazis' misdeeds. (It may even be that Streicher respected Fritz for his act of aggression. The American psychologist appointed to interview the Nazis during the Nuremberg trials heard Streicher telling a fellow prisoner that the riots taking place in Palestine had converted him to admiration for the Jews: "For such people I can only have the greatest respect.")

Whatever the reason, Fritz's avoidance of arrest on Kristallnacht was the last piece of good fortune, the last triumph, that he and his wife Anna would experience . . . unless you count the fact that they didn't die in the gas chambers.

Also in her desk was a batch of tiny, faded black-and-white snapshots taken in their flat in Nuremberg before they fled to England in 1939. She had not photographed whole rooms, only the parts of them that were special to her—a doorstop in the form of a cat, a fringed lamp on a side table, a broad window ledge with a painted vase of flowers on it. "I knew I would never see it again, I knew I might never be so happy again, so at peace, as I had felt there sometimes. So I wanted to remember it as exactly as I could."

Forbidden to take the remnants of their savings or possessions with them, she and Fritz arrived in London with literally nothing—no money, no household goods, no family heirlooms. I have a letter written by my grandfather to Fritz in June 1939, translated into English for me and my siblings by Hans. In it my grandfather talks of how Fritz had acted like a son to him, "especially in the years of my grave illness," and asks Fritz not to thank him for the money he is enclosing, "either by letter, or, the next time we meet, in speech. A handshake will do." Hans found the letter among Anna's papers after she died, and wanted us children to see what kind of man our grandfather was. At the time it was written, he said, my grandparents and Fritz and Anna were all in London; my grandparents had a tiny bit of money (though later my father would have to support them in Palestine) and was giving Fritz half of what he had—£20, a sizable sum at the time.

My grandfather's three sons had all left Nuremburg in the '30s, my father to America, Hans to what was then Czechoslovakia, Georg to what was then Palestine. Fritz, his nephew, had stayed behind. But I don't know what the grave illness was to which my grandfather referred: Had he had a recurrence of the depression that had paralyzed him when his business failed during the colossal inflation of the '20s—the breakdown that had forced my father to leave school and go to work at age fourteen? Or had he, a war veteran with a damaged arm, been beaten up in the streets again by Nazi thugs, as had happened in the late '20s? All I know is that he and Fritz were never to meet again, never to shake each other's hands.

My grandfather died before I was born, but I have a single memory of Fritz, a tall upright man who walked me, holding my hand, to a bakery near his and Anna's apartment in New York, to buy me an iced black-and-white cookie I had told him I'd seen in the shop's window. I was five years old.

He and Anna had remained in London throughout the war. At first, like sixty thousand other German and Austrian Jews, he was sent to an internment camp—the British government, in its haste to detain potentially dangerous aliens, made no distinction between Jews and Gentiles, seemingly unaware that Jews were extremely unlikely to be Nazi spies. On his release, he worked as a packer in a pickle factory and did fire-watching at night; Anna got a part-time job stringing beads for necklaces.

They barely scraped by, so the money from my grandfather must have helped a great deal.

In 1946, they emigrated to America and settled in Inwood, the largely German Jewish neighborhood where I too lived until the move to Connecticut; there they rented the same one-room apartment in which, years later, I would visit Anna. Fritz could not practice law in America with a German law degree, nor did he have the money to attend an American law school. So he got a low-paying administrative job with a charitable organization that assisted the Jewish refugees flooding into America to resettle throughout the United States, helping them to locate any relatives in the country, offering vocational training as well as financial assistance.

He and Anna had finally made some kind of life for themselves when, in early 1954, he needed a minor operation. Nobody had told them there was any danger involved, but he died on the operating table: perhaps someone had been careless with the anesthetic; perhaps his heart simply gave out. All I know is what Anna told me, which was that nothing had prepared her for his death at the age of sixty-three; more than twenty years later, the period when I visited her regularly, she was still grieving for him. They had been unable to have children, perhaps fortunately, as things turned out, but it meant she and he had been each other's world, and his death shattered that world.

"At times," she said, "that day in the hospital, the doctor coming into the waiting room to tell me Fritz was dead, comes back to me so vividly that it's as though I was living it for the first time; the loss of him hits me all over again, I am plunged into darkness." She had to struggle to regain her emotional balance, she told me, until the shock subsided, and he receded again into memory, into the photograph of him on her desk.

Yet I would never describe her as depressed; for all her melancholy, her face would often light up with joy when she was talking about the things she loved. There was a capacity for ecstatic feeling in her that I think was not unconnected to pain; it may be something that only comes after much suffering. Years later, I sensed that same quality in another woman—Lee Krasner, the widow of Jackson Pollock. With both of them, I left their presence feeling more alive, and gladder to be alive.

Anna was unlike anyone else on my father's side of the family; she was, after all, their relative only through marriage. She was more graceful than they were, light where they were heavy; she had a natural elegance none of them possessed. Even in her seventies, she was still beautiful, with deep blue eyes and high cheekbones, a delicately curved mouth, a perfectly shaped nose. She always dressed in light colors that set off her eyes and her white hair, subtly patterned pale blue blouses with gray skirts, shoes of pleated gray suede with pewter buckles. Even the coffee she served me, in tiny cups, smelled smokier and tasted richer than my own, though that might have been partly my imagination, or the cream she insisted on using, even if she was living mostly on eggs and vegetables.

She also had none of the resoluteness, the pragmatism, that characterized my father's other relations; she was more imaginative, more of a dreamer than a doer. A lover of poetry, she favored not the historical ballads of Schiller (who once said that "cold reason . . . disturbed [his] poetry") but the lyricism of Holderlin and Novalis and Rilke. She introduced the latter to me by reading his poems, in her melodious voice, in German, and then translating them for me. For one of my birthdays she bought me a paperback of his poetry in German and English, which I still have forty-odd years later. She made weekly visits to museums downtown, mostly to the Met and the Frick. (I do not think she was a great lover of contemporary art.) And she would describe to me her favorites of the paintings she had seen that week in a voice of pure elation. I think she was that rare person for whom art truly was the consolation it's so often claimed to be.

She was also a painter herself, not in her tiny apartment, which would have stunk of oil paint when she went to bed, but during the trips she took to Switzerland almost every summer after Fritz's death with Fritz's sister Sophie. (I suspect that Sophie paid for those trips, since Anna had so little money.) They were paintings of Alpine mountains and skies of Fra Angelico blue, orange-roofed cottages in wooded valleys, unmistakably European scenes. The canton of Switzerland where she and Sophie vacationed was just over the border from Bavaria, and must have looked very similar to places where she and Fritz had gone on holiday decades before. Maybe, as she was painting, she even subtly altered certain elements in what was in front of her, superimposing features she remembered on what was actually there.

And of course, while she and Sophie were in Switzerland, they would have spoken German to the waiters, the shopkeepers, the other people they met on their walks, even if the replies came in Switzerdeutsch. Though they both spoke excellent English, when they were alone with each other, I'm sure they always talked in German. It would have felt unnatural not to; it must have felt like a luxury, to settle back into their own language. (Hannah Arendt once told an interviewer what joy it gave her, when she returned to Germany to give a lecture not long after the war—and to visit her old love, Heidegger, who had briefly been a proselytizer for Nazism—to hear German spoken all around her again.)

To the children of my generation, and not just Jewish ones, German was associated with savagery: it was the language shouted or barked by the villains in a hundred war movies. And because it wasn't graceful and mellifluous, like Italian, but guttural and harsh, full of *pf*'s that sounded like spitting, it seemed only natural that it should be the language of torturers and murderers.

But for Anna, it would have carried a thousand different associations: mother, father, husband, Rilke, Holderlin, Goethe, Heine, Thomas Mann, Stefan Zweig, Feuchtwanger, Joseph Roth. The fact that the Nazis had spoken it could no more poison it for her than knowing about the Black Hole of Calcutta, or Oliver Cromwell herding Irish women and children into churches and burning them alive, poisoned English for me. None of that had anything to do with "Ode to a Nightingale."

In German, "mother tongue," like so many English phrases, is a single word: *Muttersprache*, which somehow sounds cozier, more like a caress. How did it feel for Anna, a lover of words, to leave her *Muttersprache* behind, live her life in another language? How long before she stopped thinking in German, dreaming in it? Or before she stopped feeling not quite herself when she spoke English, more like someone performing a part, as I always do when I talk in a foreign language? (If I'm speaking Greek, I use my hands more; with French, I might roll my eyes.)

There are shades of meaning, even nuances of feeling, that can't be expressed in any language but their own: some words are untranslatable. We have no equivalent in English for *Weltschmerz*, for example, or *Schadenfreude,* which is why we borrow them from German. "World pain" wouldn't convey the ache, the weariness and despair, that *Weltschmerz* does; "damage joy," as one linguist translates it, lacks the sense of glee, of pure malice, that *Schadenfreude* evokes.

There are many other German words for complex emotional states: *Fremdschämen*, to be embarrassed for a stranger. *Erklärungsnot*, misery at having to explain. *Fernweh*, the longing for faraway places, a yearning to be elsewhere. *Torschlusspanik*, the feeling that life is slipping away, time is running out. Many comic words too: *Backpfeifengesicht*, a face crying out for a slap. *Pantoffelheld*, a man who acts tough with other people but meekly obeys his wife. And my own favorite: *Verschlimmbessern*, to make something worse by trying to make it better. Every writer knows what that's like.

Unlike my father, Anna never really translated her life into English. Even Hans had worked for years in an office with Americans, took classes at Columbia in English, went to plays on Broadway. As far as I know, Anna did not watch American television; I don't remember a television set in her apartment. She listened to American radio, but only WQXR, the classical music station. She seemed to read only German books, never English ones: novels by Thomas Mann, Heinrich Mann, Stefan Zweig, the short stories of Heinrich von Kleist. (I don't know if she ever read post-war writers like Günter Grass or Heinrich Böll, but I'm sure that if she'd lived long enough, she would have loved W. G. Sebald, whose mournfully beautiful prose rescues German romanticism from its degeneration into kitsch at the hands of the Nazis.)

Nor do I recall her mentioning any American-born friend of her generation; her brother's daughter and my sister and I would have been the only native Americans with whom she had any sort of relationship. She may have read the *New York Times* occasionally, but more often it was the *Aufbau*, the newspaper for German Jews published in upper Manhattan from the '30s right through to the beginning of this century. She remained an émigré, an exile, marooned in a foreign country, in a neighborhood almost wholly populated by German Jews. Yet she had never practiced her supposed religion; she knew a great deal less about the Torah than she did about German literature.

How did she reconcile her sense of Germanness with what the Nazis had done? I have just one clue: the only time I heard of her commenting on a news story was when the My Lai massacre was reported in all the media. "You see?" she said to my sister. "Anyone anywhere can turn into a monster, even an American Boy Scout." Though she didn't say so outright, her point was clear: the capacity for cruelty was not confined to Germans alone.

For the most part, she seemed to have blotted out her memories of the '30s, so that the German *Kultur* she loved could remain intact in her mind, a Germany frozen in time; she would not allow Hitler and the Gestapo and the SS to define Germanness for her. Instead of tales of having to give up her cat and shopping at certain prescribed hours to avoid polluting the Aryans with her presence, she talked about Novalis and King Ludwig and quoted Rilke. But it's impossible to believe that those other memories didn't come back to her, at least sometimes, when she was alone, and she was alone most of the time.

Shortly after turning eighty, she broke her hip in a fall in her apartment and was moved into a nursing home, supposedly only until she recovered from the operation, but she never did go home. Somehow, the fall or the operation itself had unhinged her, as I would discover when I made the journey out to Westchester to see her, in the large sunny room she'd been given, for which Hans was probably paying. Although I'd been living in New York for the past few years, and had seen her at least once a month through all that time, she confessed to me after a few polite exchanges—about the weather, the lovely view outside her window, how kind the nurses were—that she had no idea who I was. Telling her my name didn't seem to jog her memory, so I identified myself in terms I thought were bound to clarify matters: I told her I was Rolf's daughter.

She reeled back in shock: Rolf's daughter? But Rolf had never told her he had a daughter, he had never told anyone he had a daughter. She couldn't believe it, she couldn't believe that Rolf of all people would be so

141

dishonorable, who would have dreamt it of him? To have an illegitimate daughter and keep her a secret, keep her hidden away from the world for all those years; this was *schrecklich*, dreadful, a scandalous thing to have done. At first I tried to set her straight, reminding her that she knew my mother, who had been married to my father for more than ten years, but she had no memory of either my mother or the marriage. She kept shaking her head in dismay: "People's lives, people's lives, one never really knows them as one thinks one does, there's no end to the mysteries."

It seemed the better part of valor to change the subject. So I told her, though it wasn't true, that I'd just been to see the unicorn tapestries again at the Cloisters, a place I knew she had visited many times, sometimes with me, since it was within walking distance from her apartment. Though she had not remembered my existence, she still knew some of the names of the monastic buildings in France and Spain that John D. Rockefeller had had disassembled stone by stone and reconstructed on a high cliff overlooking the Hudson. We talked about how mad and yet wonderful a project that had been, and about the unicorn tapestries themselves, and the illuminated manuscripts, and the garden: she told me the names of her favorites among the rare medieval plants and flowers it contained, describing them to me so I'd know which ones she meant.

From there we spoke of Mad King Ludwig of Bavaria, another creator of great buildings. "Poor man," she said. "He was too much of a dreamer to be a king, too shy, he wanted to be an artist, you know, and he was bullied by the Prussians, they were all bullies, those Prussians. They and the church, they both bullied him terribly. But he was a generous soul in his way, and not just to Wagner. It isn't true that he used the state's money to build those wonderful castles. Only he had to borrow too much, he got into too much debt." All this was exactly the way she'd always talked, and how we'd talked together; it seemed almost irrelevant that she had no idea who I was.

I told her, which I had hardly mentioned to anyone else, that I'd been trying to write a novel, but could not make it work. And then she quoted Rilke, first in German, then, seeing my look of incomprehension, in English: "There is only one way: go within. Search for the cause, find the impetus that bids you write." I reminded her, hoping it might be the key to unlock her memory, that she had given me a translation of his poetry. But she shook her head; no, no, she insisted, she couldn't have, after all we had never met before; it must have been someone else who had given me the book.

Which brought her back to the subject of my unfortunate birth. "You must not be ashamed of it," she told me passionately, "you mustn't let it ruin your life. Whatever the circumstances of your coming into the world, it wasn't your fault. Remember that always." So I thanked her, assuring her that I wasn't a bit ashamed of my parentage, it was perfectly okay with me, and she said that was good, that was very good, she would hate to think that I was burdened by my illegitimacy. "Anyway," she said, "children born out of wedlock are often special people, they have a special charm to them, a special grace, because they were conceived in love. I feel you are special in that way, I'm so glad to have met you after all these years. I only hope this meeting won't be our last."

But I never did see her again; two weeks after my visit, she was dead. On the wall of my bedroom I have one of her paintings of Swiss scenes, given to me by her brother when I asked for a memento of her. It is by no means great art—the perspective is slightly off in several places, the mountains look as though they're smack up against the village buildings in the foreground, but the colors are both vivid and delicate, and she seemed to have a knack for painting shadows on stone. Although the street she depicted is deserted, and looks very silent, it seems lit up from within. The faded orange door of what appears to be a municipal building glows almost eerily in what looks like more than mere summer sunlight; the sky behind the mountain is a glorious translucent blue.

CHAPTER SIX: *The Matriarch*

By the time I met Fritz's sister Sophie on my first trip to England in 1966, she had been a widow for six years; Fritz, who, with Anna, had lived in Sophie and her husband's house in London when they first emigrated, was long dead. She did not speak of Fritz to me very often—not half as much as she talked about her children and her nine grandchildren—but the last time I saw her, which she may have suspected would be the last time ever, she gave me the red-and-gold vase that had been his wedding present to her. "Bayerische Porzellankunst," it says on the base. "München Nymphenburg." In my will, I have left it to another Sophie, whom I've never met, but who, like several characters in novels I wrote after her death, was named after her.

The one time I heard Sophie raise her voice in anger was shortly after we first met. She had taken one of her American grandsons and me on a guided coach trip to Canterbury, and on our way back, the coach stopped at an inn, the guide ushered us all to round tables, and it so happened that the couple we were seated with was German, probably in their early thirties. The man of the pair was expressing pious horror about the various atrocities of English history, not only the murder of Thomas Becket in Canterbury Cathedral, which the guide had described in gory detail, but at other sites he had visited in the past few days. "I fail to understand," he said indignantly, "why the English feel so proud to show foreigners around, *zum Beispiel*, the Tower of London. It's a place of nothing but murders and torture. A monument to the shame of the English nation." To which Sophie replied sharply, "Every nation has its shame, sir!" He may or may not have recognized that she spoke English with the same heavy German accent as his own, but he clearly knew something was up; he gave her a startled look and said nothing further to us for the rest of the meal.

She might have been only marginally less indignant if he had been, say, French instead of German; she was such a passionate lover of her adopted country that she would have objected to its being criticized by any foreigner. One of the things she never forgot, never ceased to marvel at, was how, arriving in England with her husband in 1939, both of them speaking English with what must have been even heavier German accents then, she encountered almost no hostility from her new neighbors, even after the outbreak of war. "Can you imagine? If it had been the other way round, if an English couple had arrived in Germany then, this would have been a very different story."

According to her granddaughter, the reason was not entirely the amazing civility and tolerance of the English as a nation; she and her husband had moved into an upper-middle-class, very "civilized" neighborhood, not the sort of place where the neighbors threw bricks through the windows or burned down the houses of foreigners. And perhaps their neighbors, being educated people, made distinctions between Germans and German Jews that the British government did not: Sophie's younger son, who had been sent to school in England when the Nazis cleansed his *Gymnasium* of Jews, and later got an engineering degree from Imperial College, was, like Fritz, put in an internment camp for aliens, though he was released after several months and joined the Engineer Corps of the British Army. (Meanwhile her older son, who'd emigrated to America in the mid-thirties, volunteered for the American army and by a peculiar twist of fate was among the "liberators" of Nuremberg after the war. In the ruins of the town hall, he found the slashed and half-burned portrait of his and my great-grandfather and took the portrait back to New Jersey, where he had it restored.)

Unlike not just my uncle but my father and her own husband and children, Sophie's attitude toward Germany was unforgiving; she refused ever to go back, either when her husband had business there after the war, or when her younger son offered to take her to Nuremburg to revisit the places where she had been raised herself, and raised her four children. She very rarely referred, however, to her experiences in Germany in the '30s—she said nothing about the signs forbidding Jews to enter parks, libraries, cinemas, theaters; the sound of Hitler's voice coming through the loudspeakers in the public square half a mile from her apartment. The only story I heard from her was that the man who came to remove her radio once they were forbidden to Jews had worked for her husband, Otto, and apologized to her; he wished he didn't have to do this, he'd said, but orders were orders. She told me this with scorn rather than any trace of self-pity. "They were cowards, all those men," she told me, "the ones who weren't really Nazis at heart but went along. They had no backbone."

A more dramatic story was told to me by her younger daughter, the only one of her four children still living with her in Nuremberg in November 1938. On Kristallnacht, Otto was in England, meeting with the man who would soon be employing him there. Sophie was awakened by the sound of breaking glass: the SA was smashing windows on the ground floor of the apartment building where they lived. Realizing what was happening, she woke her daughter, who was sixteen at the time, and hastily bundled them both into coats over their nightgowns; then they hurried down the back stairs of the building and onto the street. After wandering through the city all night, they returned in the morning to find that most of the furniture had been smashed and the silverware was missing. Otto was supposed to be arriving from London that day, but didn't show up: though Sophie didn't know it yet, he had been arrested at the German border and taken off to Dachau.

When he hadn't returned by the next day, she took the Iron Cross he had won in the war and went to seek help from the Nuremberg police chief, the head of the SS and the Gestapo in the city, who'd been at law school with her cousin. After repeated visits from Sophie, he finally agreed to locate Otto, and six weeks later arranged to have him released from Dachau. Maybe he did it out of friendship for Sophie's cousin, but he might also have wanted to annoy his hated rival Julius Streicher, by then the Gauleiter of the entire region and the man who'd ordered Otto's arrest. (In fact, the police chief had helped several other Jews in the 30s, although later, at Himmler's behest, he had all the remainings Jews in Nuremberg deported to Auschwitz.) Whatever his reasons, shortly before Christmas the police chief informed Sophie that Otto would be on a train from Dachau arriving that night at half past midnight. She went to the station to meet him, searching the crowd of passengers who disembarked, but did not see him, and so returned to their apartment. There she found him sitting in one of the chairs whose seat had been slashed by the SA on Kristallnacht. Most of his teeth had been knocked out, his head was shaven; he was so ill and emaciated that when he got off the train she had not recognized him, while he was incapable of recognizing anyone, his glasses having been smashed by the camp guards.

Unlike his son, Otto was exempted from internment in England when they arrived in January 1939; the novel method of impact extrusion he had invented was used by the English company that employed him in the design and manufacture of shell casings determined to be vital to the war effort. By the time he died, in 1960, he was the managing director of the firm. To Sophie, this too was a miracle of sorts, another sign of the tolerance and fairness of her beloved adopted country.

Sophie never told me what Otto said about his experiences in the camp, or how much they talked about what they had both been through. But I suspect that, rather than dwelling on what had happened in Germany, Sophie chose to look forward. She probably made inquiries about dentists as soon as they arrived in England, Otto was fitted with false teeth and new glasses, and the two of them got on with things. Their younger daughter, however, was acknowledged to suffer from "nerves," a condition Sophie ascribed to the events of Kristallnacht. Instead of sending her to therapy, though, her parents chose to help her avoid stress by never demanding much of her once they escaped: she was the only one of the four children not expected to get a higher degree or go out to work. And when, later, this young woman married a particularly kindly, sunny Englishman—a Gentile—for whom

Sophie had a special affection, she considered that her daughter's troubles were over.

A few years after the trip to Canterbury, I came to London to study at University College and got a note from Sophie telling me she'd arranged to rent a television for me (televisions were often rented rather than bought in England in those days) and have it delivered to my bedsit. She deflected my thanks briskly, almost brusquely: "I am happy if you are pleased, you needn't thank me." (Both this act of generosity and her way of dealing with gratitude were typical: I am sure she not only treated Anna to their visits to Switzerland but also sent her money and practical gifts—warm underwear, woolen scarves, blankets—throughout the year, and brushed off Anna's thanks as she had mine.)

In that note about the television, she had also invited me to her flat for tea. Perhaps she felt sorry for me, or even a little curious to meet the black sheep of the family again, since Hans and maybe my father had probably given her bad reports of me. But somehow we warmed to each other that day; though we discovered that we shared an enthusiasm for English history, that wasn't the real crux of it. For all her briskness of manner, her very pronounced Germanness—she was a decidedly strong character, as fanatical about punctuality as my uncle, as scrupulous about factual accuracy as her dead engineer husband—there was also a huge warmth to her, a generosity of spirit that I responded to immediately.

Though it is usually children who are described as being bright-eyed, she had the brightest eyes of anyone I'd known—a brightness comprised partly of curiosity about everything around her and partly the cheerfulness that, though it might have been a deliberate choice on her part, never came across as false or forced. It seemed that she had decided that she could either give way to sadness or be grateful for her life. "Of course I am an optimist," she once said. "If I had thought that I would be sitting here now with my children and grandchildren, I would never have believed it. How can I not be an optimist?" It didn't occur to me then to ask her how she felt about the others, if she ever thought about the ones who hadn't lived to sit with their children and grandchildren, or the millions of children who would never be parents or grandparents themselves, their lives having ended in the camps when they were two, four, nine years old. And she made no mention of them. Perhaps, being so practical by nature, she felt there was no point in dwelling on those she could not help; instead, she concentrated on the living, giving generously to all sorts of people and charities, spending little money on herself.

She and her husband had been passionate Alpinists well into middle age, not mountain climbers but tireless walkers in the Bavarian mountains; her grown children told me of being dragged on twenty-mile hikes when they were young, and tested on their knowledge of wildflowers along the way. In her old age, she insisted on a brisk walk every day, never mind the weather. Often, before we settled down to tea and talk, I would accompany her to a park near her flat in the outermost reaches of London, and we would make the circuit of the paths together. Not only did she pick up any litter she saw on the grass, and deliver it to the nearest rubbish bin, but if she saw children dropping a candy or ice cream wrapper, she would tell them firmly to pick it up.

I knew from her two daughters that this was a habit they had begged her to give up, especially since the litterers were often adolescent boys, who might feel affronted enough to take a swipe at her or even steal her handbag. I, too, tried to convince her that it wasn't a good idea. "Look here," she told me—"Look here" and "*Ich mein*" were the preface to many of her sentences—"somebody has got to tell them, they are not behaving in a way that will let them take pride in themselves, this is very important for children." It seemed unlikely that they would regard it like that, but she could not be dissuaded, and strangely enough, nobody ever attacked her, or even told her off. Probably they were too startled at being scolded by a little old lady (she stood just under five feet tall) with a funny accent. Grudgingly, sullenly, they did as she asked, and then, rather than delivering a lecture about self-respect, which really might have been the final straw, she always thanked them warmly, she said now they could all enjoy the beautiful park together. Sometimes they actually smiled back at her.

Though we disagreed about most things—I was of course a terrific lefty at the time, whereas she was a moderate Tory—our arguments never turned rancorous; I think we both enjoyed them equally. I felt free to tell her what I thought about the war in Vietnam or my impatience with my professors' dry, joyless approach to literature, though it took me a long time to bring certain other things into our discussions, such as my feelings about my stepmother or, which seemed even riskier, the various drugs I was taking. Given my appearance, however—hair down to my waist, beaded Indian kaftans—it may well have occurred to her that I was one of those hippies everyone was always going on about. But at least I was scrupulous about showing up at her flat at exactly the appointed time.

In fact, though I was smoking a lot of hash back then, since joints were always being passed around, it mostly made me cripplingly self-conscious; I often had a better time with Sophie than with my student friends. But there was one drug I did find miraculous, acid, and having tripped on Hampstead Heath not long before, I was in a sufficient state of beatitude to try to explain it to Sophie on my next visit. It was not a mere high, I told her, it was truly a spiritual experience, I had felt at one with the universe. That was one time she did express strong disapproval, not because drugs were illegal, though she was a stickler for legality, as straitlaced in that regard as my father, but because, first, it might be dangerous: I could permanently damage my mind, or even wind up dead. "Look here, what if under its influence you imagine you can fly, you jump out the window, and break all your bones?" (That was the story about acid trips that most often made the newspapers.)

Not only that, perhaps even worse in her eyes, it was a very lazy way to seek enlightenment; it required no discipline, no hard work. "*Ich mein*, think of those people who go into caves and talk to the wild animals for years before they achieve such a holy vision." (It amazed me that she'd even heard of such people.) "It cannot be right to take such a shortcut to this religious experience you speak of, to buy it in the form of a pill." Had she been a Marxist rather than a Tory, she might have denounced the consumerist society that had turned spiritual enlightenment into a commodity, something bought and sold in the marketplace. And though I wasn't ready to concede her point about laziness, I could at least see that she had one.

While her reunions with Anna in Switzerland took place just once a year, back in London, Sophie had a friend she saw much more often: they went to the theater and to concerts together; they took a lively interest in each other's children and grandchildren. This was Rosa, the wife of Fritz's former law partner back in Nuremberg. Rosa was as energetic, as positive, as Sophie, but more extraverted, ebullient, equally sturdy but less Germanic in her manner. She had been a pampered daughter of upper-middle-class Jews and then the pampered wife of one of Nuremberg's leading lawyers, but she'd proved to have extraordinary pluck, excellent organizational skills, when they were suddenly required of her. And she, unlike Sophie, was happy to tell me about the travails and triumphs of her dealings with the Nazis.

She had chivvied the Nuremberg police chief, her husband's law school classmate, into releasing him from prison after he was arrested; she then managed, through appeals to distant relatives in California, to wrangle American visas for him and herself and their daughter. But once they escaped to England, there was no money for their passage to America. So they had to remain in London, where Rosa got her first job ever, mopping floors and washing dishes in a cafeteria. For fourteen years, while her husband was learning English, studying chartered accountancy, and finally establishing himself in a modest accountancy practice, she worked in such places, first in menial jobs and ultimately as a manager. It was the greatest accomplishment of her life, she told me, the thing she took most pride in. "And this is why I am a feminist," she said jubilantly. "You see before you an emancipated woman!"

Sophie had never been forced by financial necessity to emancipate herself from her role as wife and mother. But I wonder what she might have done if women had been encouraged to have careers when she was young. Practical as she was, she might have been an excellent engineer, her husband's profession, though perhaps, given her avid reading of books on English history, and the courses she took on the subject at the local college, she would have preferred to be a historian. Did she ever wish that she had had some outlet for her talents outside the domestic sphere? And would my grandmother have been a happier, kinder woman, a better mother even, if her father had not forbidden her to go to university, if she'd been able to exercise her intellectual gifts? Anna might have been a teacher of literature, or of art. Unlike Sophie, she had had no children to mother, no real household to run. At least Sophie had been kept busy with her four offspring when she was younger, and later, according to all her grandchildren, she played a vital role in their lives, reaping her reward in her family's devotion.

In fact, so devoted to her were they that when I wrote to her to tell her my father had died, I got a furious letter from her elder daughter in London, telling me that if I had bad news to tell Sophie, I should let this daughter know, and she would convey it to Sophie gently. I still don't believe that the death of my father, whom Sophie had seen perhaps once every four or five years, when he came to London on business, and about whose cancer she'd known from the beginning, would have been a shattering blow to her: she had weathered not only the deaths of her husband and her two brothers, but worst of all, that of her beloved older son—the one in America—who'd died suddenly of a heart attack when he was forty-eight. But when I next came to London, years later, this daughter, who had taken charge of Sophie's affairs, refused to put me on the visitors' list for the nursing home where Sophie had been moved after suffering her own heart attack at the age of ninety-four. Despite all my protests, and my assurances that I would not tell her anything distressing, she would not relent.

So although Sophie lived for another ten years, I never saw her again. I only know from her grandchildren that until she was ninety-nine, she was completely lucid, remembering the name, even, of her American grandson's wife, whom she'd met only once some years before. She was almost one hundred when her mind failed her; when this same grandson visited her three years before her death at the age of one hundred and four, she mistook him not for his dead father but for her brother Anton, who had been killed in the first months of World War I—eighty-one years earlier. It was not, then, the period of Nazi terror that her mind wandered back to in the final years of her life, but a time before that, another era of hardship and sorrow, but one in which the Germany she'd refused to revisit had still been her much-loved country, the home that when she was young she must have imagined she would live in all her life, and die in when her time came.

EPILOGUE

Sophie's younger daughter, who'd walked the streets with her on Kristallnacht, and married the kindly Englishman, brought up her two daughters in the Church of England and became a regular churchgoer herself. Alarmed by the resurgence of anti-Semitic fascist movements in Britain after the war, she even warned her children not to tell anyone about her background. But for years she led a calm and seemingly happy life, working as a nurse and then a secretary, bringing up her family and going on seaside holidays with her husband and daughters.

Then, in her early fifties, she had a breakdown, and fell into a deep depression, for which she was given not therapy but medication, which she took for the rest of her life. Years later, when she was almost ninety, she became demented. Every sound she heard in the dark outside her window was not the rustling of branches but a man in a black leather coat, carrying a gun, who was coming to arrest her. Soon it was no mere foot soldier in the Gestapo who was out there, but Hitler himself. Even in the daytime, he was watching her. People assured her, of course, that Hitler was dead, they showed her the books that described his suicide in the bunker, but she knew they were all lying, he was coming after her. When her daughters visited her in the nursing home, she interrupted the news they brought of her grandchildren to clutch at their arms and ask, "Is Hitler looking at us? Can he see us right now?" At other times, she was stricken with guilt that she was still alive, when so many of her childhood friends had been murdered: "Why am I here? Why did they let me live? Did I do something terrible?"

It was seventy years since she'd been barred from cinemas, parks, swimming pools, her German high school, since she'd been spat at and chased down the street by three of her former classmates, all of them throwing stones and screaming about filthy Jews. Seven decades since the night she'd spent walking through Nuremberg with her mother, watching the flames above the synagogues and the Jewish businesses, and going back to their apartment to find a jumble of broken chair legs, shards of china and glass, ripped books and photographs. After her father returned from Dachau, a toothless scarecrow, and she and her parents escaped to England, nobody had talked about all that, she least of all. Nobody had thought that remembering would be of any use; it was better to forget and move on.

But finally, it seemed, she had lost the knack of forgetting; all she could do was remember. The benevolent God of the Anglican church, in whom she thought she'd found shelter, had abandoned her; Hitler's was the only presence that was real anymore. Maybe, throughout her life in

England, she'd felt as though she'd been in hiding, and now she was being punished for that; the truth was out, and soon they'd be coming to finish her off.

As for the people who kept telling her, in their carefully soothing voices, that she was confused, her fears were ungrounded—look, here's the key, I'm going to lock your door and you just ring us when you want something; look, here's your daughter, she's going to stay with you tonight; look, here's the strapping young policeman who patrols the streets, he'll make sure nobody can harm you—they didn't know how easily an ax could break down a locked door; they didn't know what policemen were capable of. She had seen *Ordnungspolizei* hardly older than she was back then laughing and cheering as an old woman was dragged by her hair through the gutter; she had seen a distinguished lawyer, his face a bloody pulp, one eye hanging from its socket, being marched up and down outside a police station by two grinning men in uniform, with a placard around his neck that read, "My filthy Jew client is locked up where he belongs. I won't try to get him released again."

If her would-be comforters had been there, if they had witnessed those scenes, maybe they'd finally believe her. They might even realize that the orderly world they believed in didn't exist, there was no such thing as safety—it was innocence, not knowledge, that made them so sure they could protect her. But she was the only one who'd seen such things. And she went on seeing and seeing and seeing them until the day her heart stopped beating.

ACKNOWLEDGMENTS:

Along with my brother and sister, who generously provided me with photographs as well as memories of long-ago conversations, my extended family have helped with this book. I am grateful to Lawrence Metzger and Michael Watson for providing me with valuable information on the Metzgers, and for correcting certain misguided notions of mine about events in their family history. Special thanks to Carol Straffon, who gave me permission to use and dramatize her mother's story for the epilogue.

Chapter Three appeared, in a slightly different form, in *The American Scholar*, under the title "Uncle Hans in Exile," and in the Russian magazine *ЛЕХАИМ*.

Quotations from my Uncle George's letters, as well as certain details about his life, are taken from *The Responsible Attitude: The Life and Opinions of Giora Josephthal* by Ben Halpern and Shalom Wurm (New York: Schocken Books, 1966).

Most of all, I owe a huge debt to Joseph Olshan for his patience, intelligence, and encouragement at every step of the way. "Without whom" has become a cliché in acknowledgments, but it is certain that without him, this book would never have been written.

ABOUT THE AUTHOR

Evelyn Toynton is the author of three novels—Modern Art (published by Delphinium Books, chosen as a *New York Times* Notable Book of the Year); *The Oriental Wife*; and *Inheritance*—as well as a short biography of Jackson Pollock for Yale University Press's *Icons of America* series. Among the journals to which she has contributed are *The London Review of Books*, *Harpers*, *The Atlantic*, the *TLS*, *The New York Times Book Review*, *The Threepenny Review*, *Salmagundi*, and numerous anthologies. For the past twenty-five years, she has lived in England, on the North Norfolk coast.